The Lie Detector Man
The career and cases
of Leonarde Keeler

Portrait of Leonarde Keeler 1903–1949

The Lie Detector Man
The career and cases of Leonarde Keeler

by
Eloise Keeler

Telshare Publishing, Inc. · 1984

International Standard Book Number 0–910287–02–3

Printed in the United States of America.

Library of Congress Cataloging in Publication Data

Keeler, Eloise, 1905–
    The lie detector man.

    1. Keeler, Leonarde. 2. Polygraph operators—Illi-
nois—Chicago—Biography. 3. Lie detectors and
detection—United States—Case studies. I. Title.
HV8078.K43K44   1985   363.2′54   [B]   83–18210
ISBN 0–910287–02–3

Contents

Author's Foreword

This is a memoir of an extraordinary man, my brother, Leonarde Keeler, developer and pioneer of the polygraph. Leonarde's career, mostly in Chicago, spanned the turbulent decades of the twenties, thirties, and forties — covering the gangster era and World War II.

Apart from my own recollections, the material for the book is drawn largely from news clippings, letters, diaries, reports, and case histories that Leonarde kept in his files. Several of Leonarde's close friends and associates have contributed valuable information and anecdotes: Elwood Woolsey, LeMoyne and Louise Snyder, Lance Robinson, Ralph Pierce, and Leonarde's two secretary-assistants, Viola Stevens and Jane Wilson. Viola also helped in the selection of material. For some of the case histories and all the information on the polygraph, I have quoted Leonarde's own accounts.

ELOISE KEELER
MILL VALLEY, CALIFORNIA

Introductory
Chapter

By F. Lee Bailey Trial Lawyer and Publisher

Were it not for the "Lie Detector", few if any of you readers would have ever heard my name. Largely because of it, I have had the good fortune to appear in more different courts – state, federal and military – than any other lawyer in history. Many of those appearances were triggered by, in one way or another, my knowledge and use of the polygraph truth verification technique. I began working with the polygraph at Cherry Point, North Carolina, in 1954, where I was a Legal and Investigations Officer for the U.S. Marine Corps. Two men in the G-2 Investigations Section of the Marine Corps Air Station – Sergeant Joe Stillarty and Joe Collins, a civilian, – spent patient hours acquainting me with the theory and operation of the polygraph technique. At the same time a lawyer in Morehead City, North Carolina, where I lived, named Harvey Hamilton, Jr. taught me a great deal about the art of trying a lawsuit.

When I finished my tour of duty in late 1956 to return to civilian life and law school, I opened a private investigative agency which specialized in helping lawyers prepare their cases for trial. Occasionally, I would suggest that an attorney have his client, or one of his witnesses, tested on the polygraph to learn whether or not he or she was telling the truth. These suggestions were often met with puzzled stares as if I had advised calling in a witch doctor. I had difficulty comprehending this attitude, since in the Marine Corps we had taken polygraph testing for granted. If you were a suspect in a criminal case who took and passed G-2's polygraph test, you didn't get prosecuted, period.

I had been a member of the bar less than two months when I confronted the polygraph head-on. A seasoned criminal defense lawyer named John Tobin was defending an automobile mechanic, one George Edgerly, for the murder and dismemberment of his wife, Betty; parts of a body claimed to be Betty's had been found along a stretch of the Merrimack River, which more or less divides New Hampshire from Massachusetts. A State Police Lieutenant, in testifying for the Commonwealth, had snuck in a few remarks about the day the defendant, Edgerly, took "the tests". Defense lawyer Tobin, knowing that his client had taken a polygraph test from State Police Lieutenant Mike Cullinane, and knowing that Cullinane had deemed the results "inconclusive" took the bull by the horns: He demanded that the polygraph test results be produced. He thought, quite reasonably, that at least the jury would learn that his client had been a willing subject, a man with nothing to fear from a test of his truthfulness in denying any knowledge of the circumstances of his wife's death. In due course Lieutenant Cullinane testified that, Yes, George had willingly submitted, and Yes, the results were inconclusive. Then Frank Monarski for the prosecution sprung his trap!

An earlier test, conducted when Betty's file was labelled "missing person", not "murder victim", had been run by a pharmacist named Augustine Lawlor, who did part time work for the police at no fee. He took the stand and said that according to his test charts, Edgerly was lying. The headlines trumpeted the fact that the pendulum had suddenly swung from the defense corner to that of the prosecution. The defense team began a frantic search for someone who knew something about the polygraph. John Tobin, then 72, suffered a heart seizure over the affair. His client had forgotten to mention the Lawlor test to him, and he had walked into it headlong. The only quasi-expert the defense could find was F. Lee Bailey, 27, who was trying very hard to build a personal injury, not criminal, law practice.

I was asked to educate John Tobin so that he could cross-examine Lawlor. Tobin was too ill to understand what I tried to tell him, or to cross-examine anyone. I wound up with the task, and had little difficulty in showing that the circumstances of Lawlor's test ignored almost every rule in the book, and that it ought not to be taken very seriously. I was then asked by Edgerly, who felt that things had turned back in his favor again, to finish the case. A very skeptical judge, mindful of the fact that lawyers defending murder cases in Massachusetts are supposed to have been practicing for at least ten years, allowed me to take over; principally, as he put it, because he did not want John Tobin to die from the strain. George was acquitted amid much fanfare. My plans to try personal injury cases were postponed for a time as criminal business came flooding through my office doors.

Over the ensuing years, such famous and infamous cases as the Great

Plymouth Mail Robbery, Dr. Sam Sheppard, Captain Ernest Medina, Patty Hearst, and others have come to me at least in part because of my familiarity with the polygraph. As a result of the Edgerly case, I came to know Leonard Harrelson and Lynn Marcy of the Keeler Polygraph Institute in Chicago, and taught there for a year in the early sixties. I later taught at the Backster Polygraph School in New York. I got to meet and know a great many examiners around the country, to find out what kind of men they were (there were no women then, although there are many good ones now), what made them tick, and how confident they were of their test results on "The Box". All of this quite naturally led to a fascination on my part for the man who had really started in all, Leonarde Keeler.

I was trying a massive libel case in Las Cruces, New Mexico last February when Len Harrelson called to tell me that Leonarde's sister, Eloise, had written a biography of her brother's life and times, and would like some advice as to how she ought to go about having it published. I couldn't wait to get my hands on the manuscript to review it. Although this company had only been in business for a few months, I asked Eloise if she would trust me to publish and distribute her work. I am pleased that she accepted.

Before discussing the contents of the book you are about to enjoy, a few words about the polygraph are appropriate. Nowhere in history has the law fouled up a useful tool more dismally than in the case of the polygraph. In some ways the polygraph technique exercises a pervasive influence over legal matters, and in other respects it is branded a bastard child. Lawyers who are essentially ignorant of the true facts of the polygraph technique declaim loudly in open court that the polygraph doesn't work (when it suits their purpose to do so) and judges equally uninformed render opinions which to men and women of science make no sense. Prosecutors will announce one day that John Brown will not be prosecuted because he has "Passed a lie detector test with flying colors," and appear in court the following day to fight tooth and nail to prevent Jim Green, an accused defendant, from even taking such a test. These, obviously, are not public officials sufficiently concerned with justice. Reporters who are too lazy to thoroughly and impartially investigate the merits of polygraph testing write articles debunking a scientific method they do not understand, and the hapless public is misled. The public would be better served if it read articles by writers who had at least taken a test and tried to demonstrate the many tricks and foibles they write about, but which do not exist.

The polygraph technique is neither voodoo nor magic, and has little chance of ever replacing courts, as some highly vocal lawyers and judges obviously fear. Its capabilities are limited very sharply, but within those narrow limits it is extremely useful, and far and away the best test of credibility known to man.

Although Ms. Keeler has done an admirable job in detailing the use of the polygraph instrument in Leonarde's time (and his technique, always sound, is still in use), I will give a brief explanation of what a test is like with some of the modifications which have taken place in the thirty-four years since his death.

My reference will be to a specific examination – usually involving the commission of a crime – as opposed to the personnel screening examinations used by industry.

In order for a meaningful test to be possible, several elements must be present:

First, there must be an accusation or suspicion that you may have done something wrong, something quite specific, like taking a sum of money from a certain place at a certain time, or shooting a victim, or robbing a bank.

Second, there must be enough "Strength of Issue" to cause your autonomic nervous system to react to the accusation. Most criminal cases have sufficient "Strength of Issue" because the consequences of being branded a liar are serious. If you were asked if you lied to Aunt Tilly when you told her she looked well when in fact you thought her close to her last breath, you would probably not react because the "lie" really wasn't that important to you.

Third, there must be a proper "Distinctness of Issue" in your mind, and this is the most severe limitation on the technique. When the accusation in a question becomes at all generalized, the validity of the responses to that question diminishes sharply. Your mind must clearly know what the truthful answer to the question is, or we cannot say that your answer was untruthful. The most obvious case where distinctness is present would involve robbing a bank. One of the victims has picked you out of a lineup; you claim that you know nothing about the robbery except what you read in the papers, and were in fact at home at the time. In these circumstances, one of two situations is possible: Either you have a clear memory of being in the bank with a weapon, or you have no memory at all of the event because you were not involved. In such a case there is little chance for error if the test is conducted by a competent examiner. If however you were charged with fraudulently selling lots of land to buyers who later complained that these lots were not as represented, and you were tested on the question, "Were you acting fraudulently when you represented these lots to be valuable?", a jumble of thoughts might come to your mind, such as "I may have 'puffed' the value a bit, but that is just sales technique,", or "I really did intend to put in the improvements I promised, but the finances just didn't work out." Thoughts such as these are not sufficiently clear and "distinct" to produce a reliable result.

If the required elements are present, the examiner (the word "operator" describes an apprentice, not an expert) will collect all the known facts – called "case information" – and have an extensive talk with you. He will want to hear your side of the story and compare it with his other information in order to define the issues to be tested. This interview may take an hour or several hours. When it is complete he will go about the business of formulating the questions to be used on the test. These will be reviewed with you very carefully, for several reasons. First, it is important that the questions be phrased in a manner which you clearly understand, that there are no words in them which are not clear to you. Second, the question must be one which you feel comfortable with, one that either does or does not evoke a clear memory from the mind. And third, it is most important that none of the questions put to you while the test is running catch you by surprise; surprise questions can cause physiological reactions which have nothing to do with deception, and invalidate the test.

There are many fallacies about the polygraph, and in every gathering there will be people who profess to know how to "Beat the machine". Beware of such people. I have never met a person who can "Beat the machine," and I cannot do so myself after thirty years of acquaintance with the technique. Most do not have a clear understanding of what "Beat the machine" entails. If you will read carefully, I will educate you on this point with only a few paragraphs.

The polygraph is a simple medical instrument which monitors and records physiological phenomena occurring in the body, including changes in blood pressure and pulse, breathing, and the resistance of the skin to the passage of a tiny electrical current (one you cannot feel) over it. Blood pressure/pulse are measured by a standard SPHYGMOMANOMETER the blood pressure cuff which your doctor wraps around your arm and pumps up when you take a physical. But whereas he reads your high (systolic and low (diastolic) measurements (such as 120 over 80) by looking at a gauge, the polygraph records RELATIVE CHANGES IN

BLOOD PRESSURE on a "polygram" or chart paper, which moves under the recording pens at six inches per MINUTE.

Breathing is measured and recorded by accordion-like tubes – usually two of them, one around the chest and one around the abdominal area – which expand and contract with each inhalation and exhalation. The resistance of the skin – called "GSR" for galvanic skin response – is measured by placing two electrodes on your skin (usually two NON-adjacent fingertips), passing a minute current between them, and measuring and recording changes in the current flow as the test is in progress. When the test is completed, the examiner will have four tracings to study and interpret: One for blood pressure and pulse, two for breathing, and one for the GSR.

It is important to understand that there is no fixed standard by which these changes are measured. *You* set your own standard at the outset of the test when the examiner sets the pens on a middle level while there are no questions before you. During this time you will hear him say, "Please remain still while I balance your norm into the instrument." When he has accomplished this task, the standard as to you has been set. As the test questions are ASKED of you – and you will be thoroughly familiar with all of them before the test begins – THE EXAMINER will note on the moving chart point at which the question began, FINISHED, and the point at which you answered. Physiological reactions, or "responses" occurring GENERALLY FIVE SECONDS FROM THE POINT THE QUESTION WAS ASKED TO ROUGHLY FIVE SECONDS PAST THE POINT OF ANSWER, will be considered significant; or, if there is no response within that time-frame, that will be considered significant too.

The operation of the polygraph technique depends upon a human phenomenon which was first discovered in the 1920's, and that is the direct relation between a psychological stimulation – some condition perceived by the mind – and a physiological reaction, a condition manifested by the body. As an example, if you will recall an experience where something frightened the wits out of you, you may recall feeling a cold chill, cold sweat, or a general quavering in your voice and muscles. These symptoms were caused by the danger your mind perceived.

If someone asks you a question about some wrongful conduct which you have in fact committed, you cannot help but remember what you have done. If you admit it, you are inviting punishment. If you deny it, knowing that you are lying, you risk getting caught. During a polygraph test, the risk is that your body will give you away.

When you were a child, your body might have given you away by blushing, a clearly visible change in skin color caused by an increase of blood flow causing the capillaries near the skin to become engorged with blood, and cause the skin to flush pink or red. As an adult, the blush may not be so obvious, but the increase in blood pressure occurs nonetheless, and the instrument will measure this increase and record it very shortly after you give your answer to the accusatory question. Changes in breathing pattern and electrical skin resistance will OFTEN occur at the same time, giving the examiner a number of criteria to look at when he EVALUATES your charts.

There are two questions confronting the examiner when the test begins: "Is this subject CAPABLE OF REACTING, and "If so, does he react to the 'relevant' question, that is, the question which the test is all about?" Unless he establishes this first query in the affirmative by showing that you will react to a "control" question having nothing to do with the subject under investigation, the test will stop then and there. If you have taken drugs to "dampen" your physiological system (a dose of known drugs strong enough to cause this effect would probably make you unconscious, and would certainly be obvious), there will be no test. If you are so upset that you react to everything, that test will be discontinued until you settle down. If you are simply too tired physically to react properly, the test will have to be postponed.

If you pass this first step in an acceptable fashion, the test can continue. At this point, it becomes a rather simple exercise. If you are established as CAPABLE OF REACTION, and you do not react to the "relevant" or accusatory question, it will be apparent that you are telling the truth or at least what you believe to be the truth. You are not threatened by the accusatory question, and you are not defending against a threat by lying. If on the other hand you do react to the accusatory question, your troubles have begun. However, they could disappear within a short time.

The formulation of questions is one of the most demanding skills which expert examiners have to acquire before they are properly called experts, and if there is a single most frequent cause of invalid polygraph test results, it is because of the use of inadequately formulated questions. On a charge of bank robbery, for instance, you might be reacting MORE STRONGLY even though you had nothing to do with the robbery because you believe that your brother was involved. Until you admit this suspicion to the examiner, the reactions will persist. After you tell him, he will rephrase the question. This time he will ask, "Other than what you have told me about your brother, were you involved in the robbery of the First City Bank?" He will probably also insert another question such as, "Before you heard about the robbery of the First City Bank on the radio, did you know that a HOLDUP was going to take place?" If there are no reactions to these two questions, THE POLYGRAPH WILL HAVE CLEARED YOU OF INVOLVEMENT IN THE ROBBERY, although your brother may find himself the new target of the investigation. In short, any reaction to a relevant question can be cleared away simply by telling the whole truth about it to the examiner and then being retested. If you are guilty of the crime under investigation, telling the whole truth may result in a confession strong enough to convict you.

Now consider what it takes to "Beat the machine." You must (1) be in a healthy condition which will permit you to react to control questions, and (2) you must be harboring a guilty recollection in your memory, lie about it, and prevent your body from giving you away. Because the tie between your mind and the systems being measured – cardiovascular system, respiratory system, and galvanic skin response is the *autonomic* nervous system, you cannot control its function. The word "autonomous" means "not controlled". You might think that because you can control the inhalation and exhalation of your breath, YOUR RESPIRATORY PATTERN will not be controlled by your autonomic nervous system. The answer is, Yes, you can control the muscles which allow you to breathe, and No, you cannot control them in such a manner THAT will create a *normal* breathing pattern at the moment when you are lying to a relevant question. Your efforts to do this will not only be apparent, but will make the examiner's job easier, simply because truthful people do not try this method of covering up what their bodies are trying to say.

Most of the stories about "Beating the machine" have to do with creating false responses, not eliminating deceptive responses. If you put a tack in your shoe, you may cause responses where they don't belong, but you will not eliminate those which you must eliminate to successfully "Beat" the test and cause the examiner to call you truthful when you are not being truthful. This is why even the best examiners cannot successfully lie to one another about a significant accusatory question. I think that after thirty years of close association with polygraph testing, I would have heard of any effective means of showing up as truthful after telling significant lies during a test. The Russians would have learned it too, for no one has ever tried harder. The worst problem they have with planting agents in sensitive spy positions in the free world is the inability of these agents to pass polygraph tests.

Before you start believing stories about the inaccuracy of polygraph testing, consider the fact that the United States Government is fully satisfied of the effectiveness of the technique. You MAY HAVE read that the Reagan Administration has intensified the use of polygraph tests to contain "leaks", and to police our own intelligence agents. In a case I PERSONALLY handled, the United States Air Force bet the integrity of our Titan missile defensive system on the outcome of a single polygraph test – successfully.

The usefulness of polygraph is nothing new – beginning with the remarkable career of Leonarde Keeler; it has been with us, and functioning well, for sixty years! This account of Leonarde's growth from a bright and curious youth to a legendary man of science – the science of detecting deception, is detailed, fascinating, and persuasive. Anyone claiming to be an expert in polygraph testing who has not, within a reasonable time after publication, read this single account of how lie detection was born and nurtured, may not be an expert at all.

I know that I speak for the profession when I thank Eloise Keeler for having chronicled the life and accomplishments of her remarkable brother as no other could have done.

It has been my good fortune to become acquainted with and work with many of the top polygraph examiners in the country over the last thirty years; the temptation to mention them by name is great, but balanced against the risk of offending some top-notch examiner by inadvertent omission I will pass the opportunity. One exception, however, is my long-time mentor in the science of polygraphy, Charles H. Zimmerman of Boston, Massachusetts. I except him with a clear conscience because he has become the co-publisher of this book.

Charlie was trained as an examiner in post-war Germany by the U.S. Army, and was lucky enough to make the acquaintance of "Narde" Keeler along the way. He had achieved a distinguished reputation as a talented interrogator and polygraph examiner when I met him in late 1960. It was Charlie who recommended me to Defense Counsel John Tobin in the Edgerly case. Over the years I depended heavily on his ability to advise me as to which of my clients or witnesses was being truthful, and which was not. He has never, ever let me down.

We have worked together on this book because Charlie feels as I do – that a book chronicling the life and works of Leonarde Keeler is long overdue, and will be a vital part of the literature in the field of polygraphy.

F. Lee Bailey
Charles H. Zimmerman
Boston, MA
October 30, 1984

Excerpts from a Letter from Viola Stevens, Nard's Secretary, to Eloise Keeler — March 2, 1983

As you no doubt concluded, I could think of no case or incident where an innocent person was accused because of the polygraph examination by Nard or anyone else in all the time I was associated with Kay and Nard. That was from 1938 through 1949. I don't even recall any case where a guilty person got a pass, though there were many cases "inconclusive."

Also, I located a reprint of something Nard had published in the Yearbook of the I.A.C.P. (International Association of Chiefs of Police) for 1938–39. He says in it: "This system of diagnosis is no more infallible than other diagnostic methods. Sometimes symptoms are not sufficiently pronounced . . ." Then he goes on to say: "Exact statistics cannot be verified (regarding reliability of polygraph). Where follow-ups have been made or confessions obtained or verified, they are found to be reliable."

And further, in his own words: "In several cases brought to the speaker's (Nard's) attention, individuals diagnosed as innocent were later proved guilty, but in no case has an individual been diagnosed guilty who was later definitely proved innocent."

So there it is, from the beginning right to the end. Of course, not everyone adjudged guilty admitted it, but if anyone adjudged guilty had ever been proven innocent, it would have been broadcast and one would never hear the end of it.

I remember all the "warts", all the negative aspects of the business, and I just know there never was a case of incorrect "guilty" report by Nard. I had control of or even wrote most of the reports while I was there.

VIOLA STEVENS

Permission has been given to use all or any part of the above in "The Lie Detector Man" by Eloise Keeler.

Introduction

Leonarde Keeler was a twentieth-century genius. I first met him in November of 1948. As happened often, Keeler was called to help solve the baffling murder of a University of Colorado coed, Theresa Foster. Watching this man from Chicago, with his "lie detector," do what he was called in to do, so meticulously, had a tremendous impression on me, in fact, on my life.

Having grown up in a police or law-enforcement environment, I was knowledgeable of police investigations, including homicide investigations. I witnessed something different — Keeler with his "lie box" took the prejudice, the guesswork, the jealousy out of the investigation. Leonarde Keeler, as he had done so many times previously, solved the case for the Colorado authorities by identifying Joe Sam Walker as the perpetrator of the annihilation of Theresa Foster.

I made up my mind to get into the business of polygraph. In 1955 I would be placed in charge of running the business of Leonarde Keeler, Inc., and the Keeler Polygraph Institute in Chicago.

In looking through the records that had been compiled through the years by Keeler, I was awed by the numerous detailed notes and records that he kept on all phases of his work and readings. I still have the records and when I recall my first meeting with Keeler, it is so fitting and proper that the man who had won so very much respect and admiration from me some years before would have maintained these records. All these years later, I am fascinated every time I re-read them.

Leonarde Keeler was a keenly intelligent man. He culled

through many disciplines — physics, chemistry, physiology, psychology, language, psychiatry — to create a totally new discipline. He was suited for his work. He had a captivating personality. He was not punitive. He could get people to talk and confess their innermost, darkest secrets without Svengalian techniques. Even people who confessed to him to having committed a heinous murder would thank him afterward. He proved the innocence of many who otherwise would not have been able to do so.

Eloise, my dear friend, is to be congratulated for writing this book. She could, from Nard's records and her memories of his brilliant career in finding the hidden truth with his lie detector, write several more books.

Just as every polygraph examiner, at least indirectly, owes Leonarde Keeler a tremendous debt of gratitude (and certainly I do), I also want to say a very sincere, "Thank you, Eloise, for writing this book." Thank you, Lee, for publishing this book.

LEONARD H. HARRELSON, DIRECTOR
KEELER POLYGRAPH INSTITUTE

CHAPTER 1

How It All Started

The year was 1921. Several of us, boys and girls from University High, were at the police department in the basement of the city hall in Berkeley, California.

In a small laboratory my brother Leonarde, a tall, skinny boy of seventeen with hazel eyes rather far apart, light hair, and an ingenuous smile, sat by a strange contraption of tubes, wires, a glass bulb, and a wide strip of black smoked paper which moved on two wooden cylinders. Two metal styluses or needles were suspended close to the paper.

In a chair, strapped to the contraption by a pumped-up blood pressure cuff on her arm and rubber tubing around her chest, to record her breathing, was my best friend, Frances Chick — "Chickie".

While the rest of us looked on, Leonarde, or Nard for short, switched on the current to start the paper moving. Then, in low, modulated tones, he asked, "Do you love Harry?" There was a long pause while he watched the needles etch up-and-down white graphs on the black paper. "Do you love Ralph?" Another long pause. "Do you love Curtis?" Pause. "Do you love Henry?"

To each question, Chickie answered no. But when, in that same quiet tone, Nard asked, "Do you love Charlie?" We all burst out laughing. The needles recording Chickie's blood pressure and breathing had suddenly lurched. Blushing, Chickie admitted, "It's true. I do have a kind of crush on Charlie. But I never dreamed anybody would find out."

This was just one of many tests Nard conducted, night after night, on his school friends at the Berkeley Police Department.

He'd get them to lie about their ages, report cards, dates —
anything he could dream up. Police officers who dropped by to
watch must have been amused by these school kids invading their
domain. But it was quite legitimate. The Chief had given Nard
free rein to experiment with the strange contraption.

In those early days, we who were Nard's guinea pigs at the
Berkeley Police Department little dreamed that within a few
short years, Leonarde and his lie detector would make national
headline news; that they'd solve baffling murders and robberies,
clear scores of innocent suspects, and save millions of dollars for
banks, insurance companies, chain stores, and other businesses
plagued by embezzlers and thieves; or that they also would be
ridiculed and raise a storm of controversy that continues to the
present time.

Magazine and newspaper articles often referred to Nard as
the inventor of the lie detector. Whenever this was called to his
attention, he would explain he had developed his own instrument, the Keeler Polygraph (Greek for "many pictures"), a neat,
compact, portable instrument that he'd improved over the years.
He also started the first school for polygraph examiners and was a
pioneer in the field of lie detection. But the original lie detector,
(first called a sphygmomanometer, a name Nard had difficulty in
pronouncing; he was relieved when reporters nicknamed it
"Sphyggy"), was the brainchild of Berkeley's famed chief of
police, August Vollmer. It was built in 1921 by John Larson, a
graduate student at the University of California and one of the
chief's famous "college cops." That first cumbersome apparatus
included, among other mechanisms, a sphygmomanometer for
measuring blood pressure and a pneumograph to register breathing. For all its Rube Goldberg appearance, it worked surprisingly
well.

After graduating from medical school, John Larson went on
to important posts in the fields of medicine, psychology, and
criminology, while Nard who had assisted him with some of his
first police cases, became a criminologist who specialized in
uncovering deception.

August Vollmer, a former town marshal who became Berkeley's first chief of police in 1909, was a man of superior intellect,
integrity, and vision. Big, athletic, with graying hair, a firm jaw,
and friendly gray eyes, "he contributed as much to police science

as any man who ever lived," wrote Al Parker, author of *Crime Fighter; August Vollmer* and *The Berkeley Police Story*. Among Vollmer's many innovations were radio-equipped police cars; single-fingerprint, handwriting, and other filing systems for criminal records, including a modus operandi file to identify criminals quickly by their method of operation (precursors of today's computerized systems); a photo lab; police school; and crime prevention bureau to guide potential juvenile delinquents away from crime.

He also sought expert help from professors at the nearby University of California with crimes that were difficult to solve. By examining evidence found at the scene of a crime under a microscope, such as hairs, fibers, and soil samples, one professor supplied amazing information about the culprit: his appearance, the area where he lived, the type of work he performed. Another professor, by chemical analysis, provided other information, such as whether bloodstains were human or animal.

But despite these scientific aids, Chief Vollmer remained frustrated by his inability to tell for sure whether a suspect was lying. Watching facial expression, nervous movements and other guilty reactions such as not looking you in the eye, an interrogator might assume that a suspect was concealing the truth. But some experienced crooks could control such giveaways. And the chief would not tolerate third-degree methods to force a suspect to confess, such as beatings with a rubber hose.

Vollmer was in search of a scientific, humane way to find out whether a person was lying. Delving through literature on criminology and psychology, he learned of various methods that had been tried. In ancient China, suspects being interrogated were told to chew rice and then to spit it out. If the rice came out dry and in separate kernels, the suspect was considered guilty, for it was believed then — and has since been proven — that tension caused by guilt stops the flow of saliva.

Around 1895, Cesare Lombroso, a noted Italian criminologist, used a device developed for the medical profession to register pulse beat. Among the various suspects on whom he tried it out was a known thief; using the device, Lombroso cleared this suspect of one theft but found him guilty of another. Later the conclusions were verified.

Another more recent experimenter, D. William Moulton

Marston, studied the physical changes caused by our emotions when we lie. Most evident, he wrote in a scientific journal, was the rise in blood pressure.

Others had experimented, Vollmer found, including Hugo Munsterberg, a New York psychologist who, in the early 1900s studied the problem of lying, and Vittorio Benussi, who did research on respiratory changes as symptoms of deception. Hence the lie detector or polygraph, which today comes in various models, developed by different people and used by police departments, crime detection laboratories, the CIA, FBI, the armed forces, private investigators, and personnel consultants was actually developed not by just one or two, but by many different individuals.

But for some twenty years, until his death in 1949, my brother Leonarde was top man in the field. The Keeler Polygraph is one of three major polygraphs in use today.

Nard became acquainted with Chief Vollmer through father, a writer and civic leader who was the director of the Berkeley Chamber of Commerce in the 1920s. The chief and father had much in common in their dedication to making Berkeley an outstanding, crime-free community. Father's manuscript "Friends Bearing Torches," at the Bancroft Library at the University of California in Berkeley, tells how Nard first became interested in the lie detector.

One day, while visiting Vollmer in his office, the chief showed father a psychological chart he was preparing. Nard was recuperating from a serious operation — his gall bladder was removed — and remembering that he had expressed an interest in psychology, father remarked, "I wish Leonarde could see that chart."

"Send him in," the chief replied.

"And so, a day or two later Leonarde called on Chief Vollmer," father wrote. The chief had known him as a little boy, but had seen him only casually in recent years. Impressed by his personality and alertness, Chief Vollmer took an immediate interest in him. After showing him the chart, he took him out to see some of the department's scientific apparatus. The lie detector had immediate appeal for him. Presently father discovered Leonarde was spending all his spare time at the police station.

After several months of experimenting with Sphyggy on his

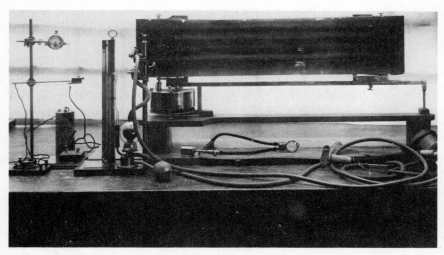

Original lie detector invented by John Larson at the Berkeley Police Department.

friends, helping in the photo lab, and making himself generally useful around the station, the Chief and John Larson asked Nard to assist them in lie detector tests on suspected criminals. Finally he was assigned his own first police case — investigating thefts at a sorority house.

The girls in a sorority near the Berkeley campus were in an uproar. They'd been missing money, clothes, jewelry, books, and other belongings. One of them had to be the thief. But which?

The house mother and several girls in positions of authority did some investigating on their own. Having heard about a word-association test taught in a psychology course, they prepared a list of words relating to the thefts; then read the words, one at a time, to each of the girls. After each word the girl was to say the first word that flashed into her mind.

Through this test, one of the least popular girls came under suspicion. After the word *money,* she said, "bills"; after *clothes,* "sweater"; after *jewelry,* "opal," and so on. Since her responses included several of the items stolen, the other girls felt positive she was guilty. She was asked to leave the sorority.

But before she'd packed her bags, the girl's parents insisted on having the Berkeley Police investigate the case. Chief Vollmer requested that all thirty-eight girls and the house mother come down to the police station. And over a period of sixteen hours, Nard, under the Chief's supervision, interrogated them on the machine.

By this time Nard had worked out a technique of interrogation. His questions were written down, numbered, and had to be answered "yes" or "no." To establish the subject's norm, he generally interspersed irrelevant or control questions with questions pertaining to the offense under investigation. Each time the interrogator asked a question, he jotted down the number at the correct spot on the graph. In most cases, the interrogator could also differentiate fluctuations on the graph caused by nervousness or anger from those indicating guilt.

Here are the types of questions Nard asked in the case of the sorority thefts:

1. Is your name Mary Jones?
2. Are you a member of this sorority?
3. Did you steal an opal ring from one of your sorority sisters?
4. Do you like sports?
5. Did you steal $120.00 from another girls' room?
6. Are you wearing a red jacket?
7. Have you been telling the truth?

The girl under suspicion was the first to be questioned. But although Nard ran several tests on her, the recording needles traced even graphs with only minor variations. The same was true for all the other girls and the house mother. Nard was baffled. Then he was told that one girl was missing.

"But you don't have to test her," the house mother assured him. "She's the president and the most popular girl in the sorority." But Nard and Chief Vollmer insisted she be brought in.

When this girl was asked if she had stolen specific items from her sorority sisters, the needles of the machine fluctuated wildly. Then, at the question, "Did you steal $120.00 from another girl's room?" the needle recording her blood pressure rose to a peak, then dropped — a definite indication of guilt, Nard was to learn in years of testing.

After the test, the girl became hysterical. But when she finally quieted down, she confessed to all the thefts. The other girls, who had thought her wealthy because of all the money she spent, were amazed. She was the last girl in the sorority they had suspected.

She wasn't arrested, but had to pay back the girls for the things she'd stolen.

Whenever Nard mentioned this case, he pointed out that while the lie detector had indicated the guilt of one girl, it had proven the innocence of thirty seven others.

CHAPTER 2

Crime Between Classes

Born October 30, 1903, in our house in North Berkeley, Nard was named for Leonardo da Vinci. Father, a writer, and Mother, an artist, hoped their son would become an artist, perhaps even like the great Italian Renaissance painter and inventor. But while Nard showed some talent for drawing, destiny had other plans for him.

Or perhaps it was Chief Vollmer who had the plans. As a boy, Nard had many interests — scouting, photography, reptiles, mountain climbing. He put on spectacular magic shows at our high school carnivals, was on the track team, played the flute in the school orchestra, and in his senior year was student body president. He seemed constantly in search of adventure. Danger exhilarated him.

His first adventure came at age two, during the 1906 earthquake. Nard and Merodine, our ten-year old sister, were asleep on an outdoor porch by the chimney, when father, asleep nearby, was awakened by loud rumbling. As the quake struck, bricks from the chimney came tumbling onto the childrens' beds. Before either was struck, father rescued them.

During the great fire in San Francisco following the earthquake, our parents helped in relief work. The strain was too much for our mother. She became ill and, in a few months died.

All our family then moved in with Grandma, our mother's mother, in her seven-bedroom brown-shingle house on Dwight Way, on the other side of the Berkeley campus. I was a year and a half younger than Nard.

Leonarde and Eloise in front of their home on Dwight Way.

When Nard was six, father set off on a three-year round-the-world lecture tour. On his return, after a short visit father took all three of us children to New York City, where he hoped to find success with his writing. Nard went to The Hackley School, a fashionable boys' school up the Hudson River, in Tarrytown, New York — my sister and I to the Ossining School for girls two towns away.

It was while Nard was at this first boarding school that he became involved in his first crime — a big one.

At school he became friendly with Lee Wilson, a boy his age, and with Lee's beautiful blond mother, who came often in her chauffeured limousine to visit her son. On several occasions, Mrs. Wilson brought gifts for all fifteen boys in the lower school. Once she hired two limousines to take them all to lunch at the old Waldorf Astoria Hotel and to the Hippodrome.

Shortly before Christmas, father, who lived in "rooms" near the theatrical district, became very sick and was unable to take his three children for the holidays. Merodine, in her late teens then, rushed to New York to take care of him. Our house mother took me to her home in upstate New York; Mrs. Wilson invited Leonarde to stay with her and Lee in their elegant New York apartment with two maids.

With their pockets full of money, the two boys were sent off each day, sometimes with the chauffeur, to explore the big city. They rode on subways and in hansom cabs, went to the zoo and skated on the lake in Central Park, lunched at expensive restaurants and attended theaters including their first talking movie with actors speaking behind the screen. For Christmas, Mrs. Wilson gave Nard a seventeen-jewel watch, his greatest treasure.

Well acquainted with the adventures of Sherlock Holmes, Nard might have done some investigating had suspicions crossed his mind while living at Mrs. Wilson's sumptuous apartment. But he was only ten. Mrs. Wilson had been good to him. He liked her.

By the end of the holidays, father had recovered and, gallant as always, called on Mrs. Wilson to express his gratitude. After the boys returned to school, he continued to see this attractive young woman. She showed sincere interest in his writing — she wanted to help him — and in his friends, particularly a multi-millionaire financier he'd met on his travels.

Gradually father began to sense something was wrong. Then he learned she was a blackmailer. She'd adopted Lee from an orphanage and put him in an expensive boys' school in order to meet the wealthy fathers of his friends. She'd found out about father's friendship with the multi-millionaire and had used Nard as a means of meeting him.

Fortunately, before father arranged the meeting, she and her chauffeur, who was her accomplice, were arrested. One of the maids turned out to be a police informer. The last we heard of Mrs. Wilson, she was an inmate at Sing Sing Prison. Lee was sent back to the orphanage.

During his New York sojourn, father had several books published and gave lectures and poetry readings. But he wasn't making much money. His inheritance was dwindling. World War

I had broken out in Europe. No longer able to pay our tuitions at boarding school, he packed Merodine and me back to Grandma in California.

In a quandary over what to do with Nard, father turned for help to Rebecca Adams, a librarian he'd met on his round-the-world trip. She arranged for Nard to live with her family in East Orange, New Jersey. Her father, Frederick Adams, was judge of the Supreme Court of New Jersey. Ella, his second wife, was some twenty years his junior. Their daughter, Nancy, was around Nard's age. He went to public school with Nancy.

Nard and Judge Adams became good friends. Evenings they played checkers. From the judge Nard acquired his first knowledge of the law and courtroom trials. From Mrs. Adams, a suffragette, he became aware of women's rights. Another of the judge's daughters by his first marriage, Constance, was married to a young actor-playwright named Cecil B. DeMille. She'd met him while performing in a play.

Meantime, in Berkeley, Grandma was having financial and health problems. She'd rented part of her house to a family — old friends of ours. Merodine, in college then, and I shared a small room there. At the end of the school year, Nard showed up and was given our former cook's room. Our changed circumstances didn't seem to faze him. He renewed friendships with his old gang and became involved in activities, mostly on the street. I was often included.

A gang of us would sneak through an unlatched window of a women's clubhouse, used only for special occasions, divide into teams, and pelt each other with pillows from the window seats. We'd chase each other over fences and through neighbors' backyards playing cops and robbers, climb over beams and rafters of partially built houses after the workmen had left, and pile onto long coasters and rattle down the Dwight Way hill. Automobiles by now had largely replaced horses. Some of our friends, thirteen and fourteen years old, were already driving. When school started, we both went to the new junior high school and Saturdays to dancing school. Nard became a very smooth dancer. He also became engrossed in hobbies. People were all around us, but Merodine was busy at the university. Grandma was bedridden, and no one really was taking care of us except Nard. Nard, somehow, felt he had to look after me.

By the following spring in 1917, America had entered World War I. Publishers were no longer interested in father's writing, and he, too, returned to California. Seeing the crowded situation at Grandma's, he realized we could no longer live there, and we moved to an adobe "studio" father had built as a refuge where he could write. It was located in a secluded canyon in the Berkeley hills, just one big studio room with outdoor porches, where we slept, a small kitchen, bath, and dressing room, but no electricity; no heat except the fireplace. But there was an acre of lush woodland with a stream running through it, and in the backyard, a shed that Nard soon converted into his "den". There he kept his camping equipment, collections and a host of creatures — lizards, snakes, rats, mice, even a tarantula. He had his own darkroom and a dots-and-dashes wireless set. One day he rushed in the house shouting, "Come out, everybody! Come out! I can hear music on my crystal set!" Two years later everyone was buying radios.

During the next few years, among other activities, father, taught English in a private school and, in 1921, became engaged to Ormeida Harrison, the assistant principal. They'd both come into a little money. He and his bride-to-be had the studio remodeled with an upstairs, bedrooms, a dining room, and modern conveniences including an electric dishwasher, new on the market. And when our elegant new house was completed, we acquired a stepmother. Her whole name was Dolly Ormeida Curtis Harrison. She wanted us to call her Mother but we couldn't. When the telephone was for her we called, "yoo hoo". But she was good to us. Nard got along with her.

It was about this time that Nard became ill and had his gall bladder removed, which kept him hospitalized for weeks and out of school for a term; but gave him a chance to work at the Berkeley Police Department. As his fascination with the lie detector increased to almost obsessive proportions, his other interests gradually tapered off. Finally graduating from high school, he took six months off to see the world, first taking short trips around California — by train when he had money, "hoboing" when broke. Then he went on a two-month voyage to Australia on the S.S. *Sonoma,* working his way as a bridge cadet. His job going over was to guard a corpse. Coming back he shared his stateroom with two large Australian pythons — boa constrictors to us — which he

Leonarde giving radio talk on his rattlesnake "diary". Snake rattled over air.

kept in our living room. When one vanished, there was near panic in Berkeley. The reporters had a field day, Nard became an instant celebrity.

That fall of 1923, he enrolled at the University of California in Berkeley, even then very large, planning to take a premed course. But Nard missed the close association with students he had had at University High. Pledged to a fraternity, he resented wearing a freshman beanie, hazing by upper class students, and the pressures to conform. His high school sweetheart, Dalthea

Baldwin, had suddenly married someone else. Two of his closest friends, Ralph Brandt, his partner on pack trips, and Elwood "Doc" Woolsey, a friend from Boy Scout days, decided to transfer from Berkeley to the University of California in Los Angeles (UCLA), then known as "Southern Branch." When a citizen's committee summoned Chief Vollmer to clean up a massive crime wave in Los Angeles, Nard decided to join his companions at UCLA.

He'd also been re-thinking the lie detector. That first machine of John Larson's had many drawbacks. It took a half hour to set up. The paper had to be smoked and was smudgy and messy. To preserve the graphs, they had to be shellacked and stored in cans, and even then they often became brittle and broke. There was much more to work out, not only with the machine, but in improving the methods of interrogation.

After moving in with Ralph and Doc in their "shack" near the UCLA campus, Nard discussed building a more practical and precise instrument. All three boys had studied physics at University High, and like Nard, Ralph and Doc had tinkered with wireless crystal sets and knew a considerable bit about electricity and mechanics.

With his two pals, Nard started to plan for a new, more compact and precise lie detector using white paper instead of the smoked paper and inked pens in place of needles. When the plans were complete, Nard took them to Chief Vollmer, now chief of police in Los Angeles. Although inundated with his monumental job of reorganizing the police department of this new, sprawling, crime-ridden metropolis, the chief was not too busy to see his chief "disciple". After looking over Nard's plans, the chief made a few suggestions, then told him, "Go ahead and build it, Nard. I'll give you a chance to try it out."

For weeks, between and after classes, weekends and nights, the boys worked on the instrument. While all this was going on the "Three Musketeers", as they'd dubbed themselves, ran out of money. According to Doc, "Nard also worked with a professional mechanic the chief had recommended. But while we all helped, Nard did by far the greater part of the work. It was definitely his invention."

Doc and Ralph flipped a coin to decide which of them would go to work. Doc won. But even with his part-time job, the boys couldn't pay for their rent, food, and parts for the machine. Father helped out with a check.

When the instrument was finally completed, Nard, outwardly calm but trembling inside, took it to Chief Vollmer. As the chief looked it over, a frown must have furrowed his brow. Years later, he confided, "That first machine of Nard's looked like a crazy conglomeration of wires, tubes, and old tomato cans. But I kept my promise."

He led Nard to an interrogation room and called for a certain suspect accused of murder. "We feel sure he's guilty," the chief told Nard, "But so far we have no proof." While they waited, the chief outlined the case, and he and Nard decided on the questions Nard would ask. Soon the suspect, the janitor of an apartment building, was brought in. As Nard fastened the blood pressure cuff on his arm and the rubber tube to register his breathing around his chest, police officers and reporters gathered expectantly outside the door.

After running several tests on the suspect and talking to him in between, Nard was convinced the man was guilty. On the graph, he pointed out to him each place where he'd lied. Nodding slowly, the suspect finally admitted, "You're right. I lied." Then, his words tumbling over each other, he spilled out his entire story.

When it was all over, the crowd surged into the room. Now it was the reporters' turn to pelt Nard and the chief with questions. Camera lights flashed. A lie detector test was big news. The police chief paid Nard twenty-five dollars and told him from here on out he could have all the cases he could handle.

That evening the three tired, hungry, but happy musketeers celebrated with a huge roast-beef dinner. As they left the restaurant newsboys were shouting, "Extra! Extra! All about the lie detector. Murder suspect confesses! Read all about it!" On the front pages of the evening papers was a picture of Nard examining the suspect on his new machine.

It was a great victory for Nard and his cohorts; also for Chief Vollmer. As there was no available office space at the police department, the chief had a jail cell fixed up as an office for Nard. To enter or leave it, he had to call a guard. Between his classes and running suspected murderers, burglars, rapists, bootleggers, and owners of gambling joints on his "emotograph" (as reporters

Leonarde Keeler as a student at UCLA with blood-pressure cuff of lie detector.

first called it to differentiate it from the Berkeley Lie Detector), Nard kept busy.

Meanwhile, father, who opposed capital punishment and challenged the need for most long incarcerations, felt some trepidations over Nard's activities. To others who, like father, may have reservations about those first cases of Nard's, I hasten to point out: even in this early stage of the lie detector, while the instruments were crude, the graphs, when interpreted by qualified examiners, were amazingly accurate. (Incidentally, that first lie detector at the Berkeley Police Department is now at the Smithsonian Institute in Washington, D.C.)

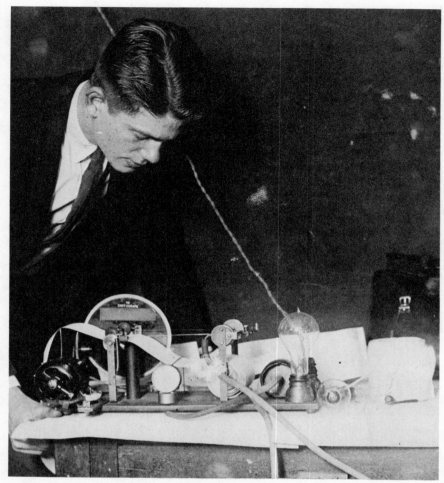

Nard with first lie detector he invented (glass bulb, wires, etc.)

Sophisticated techniques of interrogation were yet to be worked out. There was no definite code of ethics. But very soon those first experimenters Chief Vollmer, John Larson, Nard, and Captain C. D. Lee of the Berkeley Police Department, who had also developed a machine agreed on one point: no suspect should be jailed or released from custody on lie detector evidence alone. There should always be other corroborative evidence.

In October, 1932, father told Nard in a letter of a postscript to that first case in Los Angeles. While visiting San Quentin Prison, Chief Vollmer had met the janitor who was sent up for life on a charge of murder, and this convict enthusiastically championed the lie detector, even wrote the chief a testimonial about it.

"But I don't understand how a man convicted of murder by means of the lie detector could be pleased with it," father had exclaimed on hearing this.

"That's just the point," the chief had replied. "The evidence of the machine showed that he was guilty only of manslaughter, not of murder. But the jury disregarded this and convicted him of murder. He is asking that his case be taken up by the parole board. He declares that the lie detector got the exact truth and asks that its findings be used to free him."

While in Los Angeles, Nard looked up his old friend and benefactress, Ella K. Adams. Some years before, the family had moved to Hollywood. After her husband's death, Mrs. Adams had become the script reader for Cecil B. De Mille, her stepson-in-law, who was already a famous motion picture producer.

Through Mrs. Adams, Nard met Cecil's brother, William De Mille, also a movie producer, his wife, Anna, and their two daughters, Agnes and Margaret. Agnes went on to fame, first as a dancer, then as the choreographer of such musical hits as *Oklahoma* and *Carousel.*

While Nard was at UCLA, Agnes was also a student there, and she and Nard became good friends. Telling of her college dates in her book, *Dance to the Piper,* she wrote, "I was also having dates with Leonarde Keeler who was working out campus thefts and misdemeanors on his lie detector."

Nard, Ralph, and Doc were all invited to Sunday night suppers at the William De Milles' big house on Hollywood Boulevard, where they met famous writers, producers, directors, and some of the top movie stars of that era, including Charlie Chaplin, Douglas Fairbanks, and Mary Pickford. All were intrigued by the lie detector and by Nard's dramatic tales of crime and criminals.

The boys had been in Los Angeles only a few months when, through faulty wiring, their shack caught fire and burned to the ground. All their possessions, including the lie detector, were destroyed. In a letter to me soon after the fire, father reported that already Leonarde had rebuilt his machine, with improvements, and just as soon as it was completed, the L.A. Police Department had called him on a case. A pistol used to shoot a policeman, and money collected for the policeman's widow, had been stolen from the desk sergeant's locked drawer. Father didn't know the outcome of this case but said Nard must have solved it, for he was continuing to work on cases for the police. I later learned that out of 125 possible suspects, Nard had picked the guilty man.

After a year in Los Angeles, Chief Vollmer had completely reorganized the L.A. Police Department, dramatically reducing crime, and introduced police cars, traffic lights and many other improvements. He decided to return to Berkeley to finish his work there. As if on cue, those Three Musketeers, Nard, Ralph, and Doc, transferred to Stanford University in Palo Alto, some forty miles south of San Franciso.

Despite Nard's success with the lie detector, he still planned to become a doctor. His uncle, Dr. Sterling Bunnell, whom he greatly admired, had promised him a place in his office. And he resumed premed studies at Stanford. But again there were distractions.

The three boys lived in a cottage behind the Stanford campus. On the property was an abandoned water tower that may have inspired Nard to start a unique business, with Doc as his partner. They called their offbeat enterprise a "rattlesnake dairy." The snakes were kept in cages on the second floor of the water tower and were "milked" of their poison by the ambitious partners, who sold it for a good price to the Cutter Laboratories in Berkeley to be used for anti-snake bite serum.

In addition to his regular classes, Nard also took flying lessons, and, winters, he and several buddies went on perilous snowshoe trips in the high Sierras. But his predominating interest was still the lie detector. He kept in close touch with Chief Vollmer in Berkeley. He even got his experimental-psychology professor, Walter Miles, and the whole class into the act.

While at Stanford, he made additional improvements on his instrument and techniques of interrogation. In a magazine article he explained: "This new instrument records quantitative changes in systolic pressure. We can now say that a certain stimulus gives a response of 10mm. of mercury, etc. This method of obtaining blood pressure records is far superior to an instrument that merely indicates that a pressure change has occurred without indicating how much."

Around this time, Chief Vollmer took Nard and the newest model of his handmade lie detector to Oakland to call on Bill Scherer, head of the Western Electro Mechanical Company, Incorporated. Following Nard's plan and written instructions, Mr. Scherer developed a mechanical metal bellows, a motor drive, a pneumograph to go around the chest, and a mechanical indicator to mark the graph when a question was asked. This first professional lie detector (the term "emotograph" had been dropped; polygraph not yet adopted) was neatly encased in a mahogany box that looked like a traveling case. "In the next few years we sold sixty to eighty of them to police departments in California and all over the country. One was shipped to Honolulu, several back east," Scherer recollected decades later.

Nard and Professor Miles also developed a blood pressure pump, used for a time at Stanford Hospital to monitor the blood pressure of patients undergoing surgery. It, too, was manufactured by the Western Electro Mechanical Company.

With several classmates, Nard conducted lie detector experiments at the U.S. Veterans Hospital in northern California. Of these early experiments, he wrote:

"Startling characteristics of records obtained from various types of psychopaths were observed. At present this phase of pneumocardiosphygmomanometer experimentation is held in abeyance until further developments are added to the machine."

At Stanford Nard worked out a card test that, over the years, he used to demonstrate the reliability of the lie detector. Fanning out ten cards, he'd tell the person attached to the machine to pick one. "Don't show it to me. Just look at it and put it back." Shuffling the cards and instructing the person to answer no to each question, Nard would hold up the cards one by one, asking, "Is this the card you took? This? This?" and so on through all ten. Afterward he'd tell the person which card he'd chosen and show him on the graph where he'd lied. This test was practically infallible.

Since his first case for the Berkeley Police Department screening the girls at the sorority house, Nard had been asked to run tests at various college dormitories, both at UCLA and

Stanford, where valuables had been reported missing from students' rooms. When it was announced ahead of time that he and his lie detector were coming, money, clothing, books, and fountain pens often mysteriously reappeared.

In another state, at a law school library, more than two hundred books were discovered missing. Apprised of the theft, the student council summoned all 350 students of the law school to a meeting. The president of the council, who knew of Nard's experiments at Stanford, suggested that all 350 students submit to lie detector tests. Only the guilty had cause to fear, he insisted. Such tests also would familiarize the law students with one of the newest types of equipment in crime detection.

The students debated the proposal. Some protested that their constitutional rights would be violated, a complaint that has been voiced many times since. On a final vote, those in favor of the tests won, however, and Nard was called in.

After he tested twenty-four young men and women students who worked in the library, feelings became so strong against the use of the apparatus that all subsequent tests were called off. The results of the tests already given were kept secret. Then, in the next few days, as though by magic, almost all the missing books reappeared on their shelves.

This was not the only occasion Nard was called from his classes to run "suspects" in other localities. Police chiefs, sheriffs, and attorneys wanting lie detector tests called Chief Vollmer, who in turn recommended Nard. These cases ran the gamut from petty theft to homicide. The Berkeley Police Department issued Nard a license to carry a concealed weapon for "self-protection while traveling." The chief arranged for his leaves of absence from college.

CHAPTER 3

What Makes Criminals Tick?

In the summer of 1927, still a student at Stanford, Nard was sent to Chicago on an unusual assignment. In this instance, it didn't directly involve the lie detector.

Three years before, two brilliant young men from wealthy Chicago families, Nathan Leopold, Jr., nineteen, and Richard Loeb, eighteen, set out to test their intellectual superiority by committing the perfect crime. Showing no compassion or moral inhibition, they callously murdered nine-year-old Bobby Franks, a neighbor, and left a ransom note for his parents. Soon caught, the murderers were brought to trial, defended by Clarence Darrow, the famous trial lawyer.

This senseless crime shocked the nation. A macabre climax to the "flaming youth" era of blaring saxophones, hip flasks, and joy rides that followed World War I, the crime particularly alarmed parents of adolescent youngsters as well as community leaders throughout greater Chicago. Many concerned citizens contributed to a behavior research fund which was used to finance the Institute for Juvenile Research. In addition to investigating causes of behavior in juveniles, the institute, directed by Dr. Herman Adler, state criminologist, also arranged for qualified young men to tutor adolescent boys in need of professional guidance.

While on a trip to San Francisco, Dr. Adler met Nard through Chief Vollmer. Interested in Nard's work with the lie detector, Adler asked him to help out that summer by working with one of these boys.

The boy Nard tutored was attractive, basically bright, but

was having difficulties with his studies and his relations with other boys. He was afraid of girls. He and Nard liked each other. After a few weeks of getting acquainted, with the family's permission and using one of their cars, Nard drove the boy across the continent to Berkeley. En route he took him camping in the Sierra Nevada. The boy went wading and fishing in clear mountain streams, helped prepare meals over a campfire, learned the names of birds and flowers, and soon shared Nard's enthusiasm for the wilderness. Along the way Nard took him to several country dances. Girls began to interest him. And by the time Nard got him back to Chicago, he was a changed boy. The boy's father wrote of his gratitude and told of his son's progress in school and in social relations.

During his Stanford years, Nard dated numerous girls. No longer the skinny schoolboy, he had filled out, was quite handsome, and bore himself like a leader. After his engagement to a coed from his psychology class fell through, Nard took a fancy to Katherine ("Kay") Applegate, from Walla Walla, Washington. Tall and well built, with light, wavy hair and rosy cheeks, Kay had an aloof dignity. Her slow way of talking and sudden shifts in mood were intriguing. But what particularly appealed to Nard was her love of adventure.

One summer she and Doc Woolsey's girl friend, another Katherine, after trying unsuccessfully to get jobs on an ocean liner to Hawaii, stowed away by mingling with the passengers. As it would have been too expensive to send them back on another ship, the skipper, a friend of Doc's, allowed them to continue to Honolulu. There they found jobs, first flipping pancakes in the window of a restaurant, then working in a pineapple-processing plant. Kay also took flying lessons in a World War I Jenny, and both girls sold articles about their adventures to newspapers.

This caper amazed Nard. He thought Kay the most fascinating girl he'd ever met — beautiful, intelligent, daring, unique. But despite his newfound love, in the summer of 1929 he left Stanford to take his first full time job using his lie detector. It was at the Institute for Juvenile Research in Chicago.

During part of the year Nard worked for the Institute, he spent five days a week examining prisoners on the lie detector at the Illinois State Penitentiary at Joliet. He wrote me a remarkable letter:

> ... Dr. Adler, the state criminologist, brought me out here to the penitentiary the Monday after I pulled into Chicago. My office had to be built in the Mental Health building and is now completed. The blood-pressure apparatus is set up and already a half dozen prisoners have been run on my various tests.
>
> I occupy a large room in the Warden's quarters — have a double bed and all the conveniences of a high-class resort hotel. The cleverest burglar Chicago has ever had is my valet and room boy. He keeps the room in beautiful shape, my laundry out, and sees that my suits are pressed. On the side he's writing his life history for me. When not busy he sits at a table in my room and scribbles off his most exciting jobs.
>
> I eat at the officer's mess and am waited on by a young fellow who is in for theft. Then down the corridor is the barber shop. The barber who shaves me every day and keeps my locks trimmed up, is a nice kindly fellow who raped his daughter.
>
> In the office three "trusties," in for forgery, larceny, and embezzlement, are secretaries, and we have a young porter who's in for murder. But he's a nice little fellow at that ...
>
> "Dickey" Loeb is a runner for the deputy warden, so he comes into the office each day, and we're becoming quite well acquainted.
>
> Today I went to Chicago to give a lecture on crime detection before a class at Northwestern University Law School, and after lunching with the dean at his club, came back to Joliet. My researches here pertain to the integrity of the convicts and to their reactions to their childhood life, their criminal career, and their prison environment. I have four different tests that I'm going to give to about a thousand convicts. From this date I'll attempt to discover why they went crooked and the probability of their going straight when paroled. If we can devise a reliable test showing which ones will be good citizens when released, we'll have a means of informing the parole board which ones to let out and which to keep. If the results here show anything I'll then be transferred to Chicago to work on children at the Juvenile Court ...
>
> Got a letter from Kay Applegate saying she's quitting Boeing Airplane Co. and coming to Chicago to get a job in some psychology work. Gosh! I don't know what this means. It looks bad. I'm afraid I'll be responsible for her here — and that might lead to most anything. I'll have to take her to New York so you can pass judgment.

A few weeks later Nard wrote again. Kay had arrived in Chicago and had gotten a job in "psychology work"—at the Institute for Juvenile Research.

Since the purpose of the questions Nard asked the prisoners at Joliet was not to incriminate them, many talked freely. Some even told him about crimes they'd committed other than the ones for which they were serving time. Although many of the hundreds tested claimed to be innocent, Nard was convinced that two were telling the truth. He talked over their cases with prison officials. Soon machinery was set in motion for their release. As in previous cases, lie detector evidence alone was not sufficient to free them, but it did influence authorities to investigate their cases. When these two prisoners were finally freed, Nard and his lie detector received national acclaim. Not only could this strange new device catch criminals, it could prove the innocence of men unjustly convicted.

During his time at Joliet, Nard invited me to come to Chicago and share an apartment with Kay. I accepted. Although I hadn't known Kay before, we got along remarkably well. We lived at an apartment hotel near the University of Chicago.

Over weekends, Nard and Kay often invited friends from the institute for little supper parties, or we'd all be invited to someone else's place. As it happened, Chief Vollmer was then teaching a class in criminology at the University of Chicago, and he and his attractive wife, Pat, came to many of these affairs. We started calling Chief Vollmer just "Chief," and he and Pat, who enjoyed younger people, became our close friends. It was a rare privilege getting to know them on an equal footing. After all, the Chief had been written up in *Collier's Weekly* as "America's Number One Cop".

Besides reorganizing police departments in various cities, serving on President Hoover's Crime Commission, teaching a course in criminology to police chiefs from all over the country, the Chief studied psychology ardently and had a rare insight into criminal motives. He told me once that if he had the same ancestors, the physique, background, education, and experience as a bank robber, he also would probably rob banks.

Conversation at these parties centered on the most recent theories in psychology and criminology. We even carried on experiments with word association tests and Rorschach tests—

studying ink blots, then telling what they resembled — a butterfly, a bat, a skull, and so forth. And we had many discussions of the then-revolutionary theories of psychologists like Freud, Adler, and Jung. Terms like the subconscious mind, sexual repression, dream interpretation, the libido, id, dementia praecox, paranoia and psychoneuroses were new to me and seemed a bit scary. Once when I complained of feeling blue, Kay suggested half-humorously, "Maybe you're a manic-depressive." Nard laughed. "What she needs is a man." Next thing I knew he'd invited Bob Echols, my beau in New York, to come and visit us.

Bob stayed a few days. Nard liked him. A mathematician and physicist, he was also extremely good looking, with reddish wavy hair, brown eyes, and an engaging Southern accent.

Weekends, when Nard was in Chicago, he'd tell us about his work at the grim, fortress-like penitentiary. The severe punishments inflicted on the men for petty infractions of the rules disturbed him. He recommended a new type of merit system, in which a definite numerical value would be affixed to each violation — i.e., attacking the keeper (15); fighting with fists (20); planning a riot (100); refusing to work (10); faking illness (10); and so on. He also believed that the merit system should give credit for good behavior and that inmates should have a center or bureau to which they could apply for help with their present and future welfare. And he explained the social benefits of the lie detector in the prison setting:

> In my short tenure here I have found that if the examiner puts himself on the same social level as the inmate being interviewed, holds out a helping hand, and indicates by his attitude, gestures, and words that he wants to help, the inmate loosens up and talks more openly about his case. Under these conditions a great majority of the men interrogated on the lie detector confess to their crime, which, before, they'd claim was a bum rap. After confessing, the prisoner's conflicts, secretiveness, and dishonesty become things of the past. The man feels consciously that he has a clear record. He can be more frank and honest about his present, thus enabling the prison psychiatrist to give him greater help and incentive.

In the years that followed, many former inmates and guards Nard had befriended and tried to help kept in touch with him.

Like workers in related fields, Nard found that many of the prisoners were disturbed. As children they'd been unwanted, neglected, or abused by adults. Some lacked schooling or were mentally defective. Others were ill, addicted to drugs or alcohol, or physically abnormal. Nard used to tell about a very ugly criminal who, after plastic surgery, became an honest, law-abiding citizen. Indeed, the majority of men behind bars, he found, were in most ways not so different from the rest of us.

Years later, after testing thousands of employees of banks, businesses, chain stores, and other organizations, Nard discovered more direct and startling causes of crime — and also an unusual means of keeping people honest. But in the late 1920s, while he and his intellectual pals were trying to figure out what made criminals tick, crime in Chicago was flourishing as never before. Sinister-looking henchmen of "Scarface" Al Capone and other bigtime gang bosses were taking members of rival gangs for "rides," shooting up joints with sawed-off shotguns, and vandalizing firms that refused to ante up protection pay. Some of the bosses owned brothels or gambling concessions. Some trafficked in dope. Most were bootleggers, supplying booze to politicians, business magnates, and almost everyone else. Because mostly they only shot down each other, the general policy seemed to be to leave them alone.

Looking back on that period, it seems to me now that while Nard had carried on hundreds of experiments with the lie detector and had worked on numerous police cases during his college years, he was still waiting in the wings. The stage was set, the actors ready, but the curtain had not yet risen on the big show.

Several months before Nard left Stanford to take his new job with the Institute for Juvenile Research — on February 14, 1929, to be exact — seven gangsters were waiting in a garage on Clark Street for the delivery of a truckload of booze, when a big black car pulled up in front. Five members of a rival gang, two disguised as policemen, got out. As though on a raid, they strode into the garage, lined up the seven men against a wall, and blasted them with machine guns.

The St. Valentine's Day Massacre convinced two leading Chicago businessmen, Burt A. Massee and Walter A. Olson, that gangsters had gone too far. Massee and Olson put up money for the first scientific crime detection laboratory in the United States, which was to be affiliated with Northwestern University.

The following year the laboratory, on Ohio Street in downtown Chicago, was ready to open. August Vollmer was a consultant on the project. Nard was among the experts hired to man it. War on crime had been declared.

CHAPTER 4

Science vs. Crime

Soon after Nard left the Institute for Juvenile Research to join the new Scientific Crime Detection Laboratory, Saturday, August 16, 1930, he and Kay were married. Judge Henry Horner of the Chicago Probate Court, a friend of Nard's, performed the ceremony at the Chicago Lake Shore Club.

As Nard's services as a lie detector examiner were already in demand, the couple didn't take time off for a honeymoon but moved directly into a modern two-bedroom apartment on Chicago's West Side. Soon, Kay left her job at the Institute to become secretary to Col. Calvin Goddard, director of the crime lab, and an expert on firearms and ammunition.

Colonel Goddard was chosen for this post by Burt A. Massee, a wealthy Chicago businessman who had served on the coroner's jury of the St. Valentine's Day Massacre. At the autopsy, physicians had extracted forty-six projectiles from the seven victims. Some twenty other bullets had missed.

The crime was so appalling, so vicious, that Massee and Walter A. Olson, another businessman on the coroner's jury, determined that its perpetrators should be tracked down and an end put to gang warfare and violent crimes. Hearing about Colonel Goddard, who had received acclaim for his work on the Sacco-Vanzetti case, they asked for his help. Colonel Goddard was able to show that all the projectiles used in the St. Valentine's Day Massacre had been fired from Thompson submachine guns and shotguns, weapons not used by the Chicago police, thus clearing the police of any suspected complicity. Goddard's knowledge of firearms and his scientific methods of investigation so

impressed Massee and Olson that they commissioned him to set
up a scientific laboratory for crime detection in Chicago that
would not be involved in politics.

After consulting experts on criminal investigation in this
country, Colonel Goddard crossed the Atlantic to confer with
criminologists and study laboratories in London, Paris, Berlin,
Copenhagen, Rome, Brussels, Vienna, and other European cen-
ters. At that time, scientific crime detection was more advanced
in Europe than here.

On his return, Goddard set up the first scientific crime
detection laboratory in the United States affiliated with and
administered by Northwestern University and supported by private means (mostly those of Burt Massee) at 469 East Ohio Street
(and later at Superior Street) in Chicago. Its services were offered
"to police officials and all other persons anywhere who desired
expert analysis of the physical traces of crime." Massee became
president of the corporation; Olson, vice-president. Dana Pierce,
president of the Underwriters Laboratory, was treasurer, and
John H. Wigmore, professor of law at Northwestern, became
secretary. All were united in their belief that "without law,
property is only a word; without security there is no property."

The laboratory was spacious, covering an entire floor, with
offices in front and a shooting range in the rear. All the men
employed there were trained in the use of firearms. The full-time
staff included experts in firearms' identification and explosives,
photography, microscopy, photomicrography, applied physics
and chemistry, toxicology, document examination, moulage
(making casts of objects such as tire-tread marks), and Nard's
special field — psychology and deception tests. (Nard also was on
the medical faculty of Northwestern as research assistant in
psychology.) In addition to the nine full-time staffers, an associated staff of experts could be called on as needed in fields such
as criminal law and administration, medical aspects of crime,
incendiarism and arson, burglar-resistant devices, gems (real
and spurious), and decoding.

But rather than go into more detail about this first fully
staffed and equipped crime detection laboratory, which was to
serve as a model for similar laboratories across the country, I'll let
Nard explain in his own words how he and other experts solved

specific crimes. The following cases are culled from notes Nard
prepared in 1933 for various articles, lectures, and radio talks.

Some years ago, in the state of Washington, a school girl on her
way home through the woods over a lonely trail was brutally
assaulted by some stranger who had jumped from behind a blind
made of fir boughs. The police of the district were immediately
called and worked for some days following scanty clues that were
suggested by the girl. At the end of a week, the girl was still unable
to identify anyone as her assailant, and it seemed that the police
had reached the end of their trail in the solution of this crime.

However, an expert in crime detection methods was called in to
examine all the evidence. He found only one real clue. The boughs
of the blind behind which the assailant hid himself were cut from
living trees with a knife. The scratches made by the minute
irregularities in the blade of the knife were easily visible under a
magnifying glass.

The authorities finally apprehended four or five individuals who
might have been capable of committing such a crime. Each was
requested to turn over his pocket knife to the investigator in
charge. In turn, each pocket knife was used to cut twigs similar to
those used in making the blind, and each twig was photographed
with the aid of a microscope so that every little defect in the knife
blade, reproduced on the cut surface of the twig, was easily discern-
ible. These photographs were finally matched up with photographs
taken of the twigs used in constructing the blind, and it was found
that the scratches made by a knife belonging to one of the suspects
matched the scratches on the twigs used in the blind. The actual
evidence, along with all of the photographs, was presented to the
jury in the trial of the suspect and he was convicted. The case later
went to the Supreme Court of Washington, which affirmed his
conviction, and in the court's opinion, we find this statement:

Courts are no longer skeptical that, by the aid of scientific
appliances, the identity of a person may be established by
fingerprints. There is no difference in principle in the utilization of
the photomicrograph to determine that the same tool that made
one impression is the same instrument that made another impression. The edge of one blade differs as greatly from the edge of
another blade as the lines of one human hand differ from the lines
of another. This is a progressive age. The scientific means afforded
should be used to apprehend the criminal.

In almost every police case, there is some evidence that may lead to the apprehension of the criminal providing it is examined by trained individuals. Science is progressing so rapidly today that it is difficult for most of us to keep abreast of the times. We have electric lights and appliances, airplanes, submarines, radio, and a host of other things that at one time almost everyone said were impossible. And we shall continue to have inventions and discoveries equally unbelievable. We shall find new methods for doing old things, but mankind will continue to doubt.

When the fingerprint system for identification was first established, the public and the police scoffed. Between the time that Galton first showed that all fingerprints were dissimilar and the time fingerprint evidence was accepted in court, eighty years elapsed. Now the police consider the fingerprint system indispensable, and the layman has no doubt as to its dependability. The criminals know how effectively it functions.

When the police radio system was first suggested for the City of Chicago, some of the commanding officers scoffed at the idea. Now that the police radio system has been in use for a number of years and has been responsible for thousands of arrests, these same officers say, "We couldn't do without it."

At one time, photographs were inadmissible as evidence in court, and even after photographs were admitted, X-ray pictures were banned, but now they, too, are accepted as reliable evidence. Handwriting testimony given by an expert is readily accepted in court. Experts in firearms identification testify as to which gun fired a certain bullet, and scientists in numerous other fields are called on to examine bits of evidence and give their testimonies in court which may help prove the innocence or guilt of a suspect.

Here in Chicago, a seven-year-old boy was run over by a hit-and-run driver who fled and escaped in traffic. Witnesses obtained part of the license number of his car, and investigators immediately set out on his trail.

Several cars that answered the description of the hit-and-run driver's car were located and examined for clues. On the various cars, all of the headlight lenses were intact, but under examination with ultraviolet light, it was revealed one pair of headlights had two different types of glass. The lens from one light fluoresced one color, and the lens from the other light fluoresced different color, indicating a dissimilar type of glass. It was evident from this that the car in question had, at one time, a broken headlight lens which had since been replaced.

Further examination of this car revealed, under the front fender, one hair and two tiny threads. These bits of evidence were carefully scrutinized by a competent microscopist, who found the hair to be from a human being. This single hair, compared with known hair of the deceased, was found to have the same pigmentation and other characteristics and to have on it a certain type of industrial dust. The boy had lived near a graphite factory and his hair had been filled with minute particles of graphite.

On the two tiny threads found with the hair was revealed a trace of human blood which couldn't have been seen with the naked eye. Under the microscope, the threads appeared identical to threads taken from the boy's clothing. It seemed there was no doubt that the killer's car had been found. When all the findings were presented to the suspect, he admitted that he had run over the child.

Had it not been for the microscopist who examined the threads and the hair, the chemist who determined the presence of human blood, and the physicist who discovered the difference in the headlight lenses, this hit-and-run driver would probably not have been apprehended.

Nard stressed, "At the scene of a crime, nothing should be disturbed until highly trained investigators have made a detailed examination of the entire surroundings and have carefully preserved, recorded, and photographed any traces of evidence to be examined later by experts in a scientific laboratory."

About his own department at the crime lab, Nard wrote, "Here, too, we have methods for the examination of suspected individuals to determine their connection with certain crimes — a modern scientific procedure, the antithesis of the old third degree method for determining truthfulness."

As an example of his particular role, he told about the brutal double murder of an Ohio farmer and his wife.

Their bodies weren't found for almost a month after their deaths and practically no clues were uncovered by the investigators. The approximate time of the murders was determined by the autopsy and the fact that newspapers delivered to the mail box had not been picked up after a certain date. Neighbors recalled seeing a young farm hand walking across the couple's property on the date established for their deaths. But when this boy, Chester Smith, was questioned by the investigators, he denied any knowledge of the crime and claimed he hadn't been near the house of the murdered couple on that day.

Doubting his truthfulness, the investigators took him to the crime lab in Chicago where, with the boy's consent, Nard tested him on the lie detector. Before the test, Nard showed him a list of names of all the people who lived within a mile or two of the scene of the crime. Then, during the first test, while the boy's blood pressure, pulse, and respiration were recorded continuously on a moving strip of paper, Nard asked, "Did Jones have anything to do with the murder? Did Mr. Stone have anything to do with the murder?" and so on down the complete list. Chester responded, in his blood pressure specifically, to the names of two individuals, a farmer named Miller and Clyde Bourne, a young farm hand who at one time had worked for Miller.

In another test, Nard questioned Chester on whether he had any direct knowledge of the crime. To each question, the boy responded with observable blood pressure and respiratory changes, indicating that he was a participant in the murder and that the other two individuals were also implicated. On completion of the tests, Nard showed the boy the changes on the graph in his blood pressure and breathing, indicating his responses to certain questions. Aware that his lies had been revealed, Chester then made a full confession. Farmer Miller had paid him and Clyde, his farm hand, twenty-five dollars each to kill his neighbor and his neighbor's wife. Apparently, Miller had been responsible for burning down some of the neighbors' barns. The deceased farmer knew about Miller's activities and had threatened to expose him. For this reason, Miller decided he had to get rid of both the neighbor and his wife. The two farm hands pleaded guilty to the murders. Miller was given a life sentence.

This was just one of some four thousand lie detector cases on which Nard and his assistants worked, an example of the scientific methods used at the lab. Most of the cases taken there by the police, sheriffs, and district attorneys were hard to break. And while the men who peered through microscopes, tested chemicals, compared handwriting, photographed evidence, made plaster casts, and ran endless tests on the lie detector, were generally serious-minded and engrossed in their projects, an air of challenge and excitement permeated the lab. This was accentuated by the sound of shooting, occasionally by the rat-tat-tat of machine guns, when these men of science took their required practice at the lab's shooting range.

CHAPTER 5

The Telltale Galvanometer and Truth Serums

In December, 1930, Nard wrote the following report on his various activities at the crime lab:

Most of my time has been consumed in testing suspects of crimes, examining the personnel of banks, and conducting research with the polygraph. Incidentally, I have experimented with the filtered ultra-violet ray and have made several examinations of evidence with the aid of the lamp. Also, I have experimented considerably with etching solutions in restoring obliterated numbers on guns, and in time of necessity have substituted in making examinations of objects (evidence); of blood, semen (in rape cases), and foreign particles such as hairs, fibers, and dust.

Have also given a number of talks and demonstrations on the activities of the laboratory with detailed explanation of the deception test technique.

TALKS

Lectures on the work of the laboratory and demonstrations have been given as follows:

N. W. Univ. Law School - Dean Wigmore's class

Three demonstrations - Police School (Detective Bureau)

One demonstration - Police Lieutenant's Assn.

One demonstration - State's attorneys

Univ. Chicago - Chief Vollmer's class

Symposium - Scientific Crime Detection Lab

Lakeview Lions' Club

Logan Sq. Medical Assn.

Sequester Club

Yale Alumni — Class '96

International Bureau of Personnel — Madison, Wis.

International Bureau of Personnel — Chicago

Forum Club of St. Louis

City Club of Chicago

Int'l. Assoc. of Identification — Miami, Fl

Legal Club of Chicago

Womens' Aid Society — Chicago

CASES

The criminal cases I have engaged in while a consulting member of
the staff as well as regular staff member are as follows:

Canary Murder (victim was canary)

Bank Robbery

Black Creek Bank Robbery

Western Hotel Murder

Lake Forest School Thefts

Lee Rape case - Des Moines, Iowa

Divel Murder case - Sharon, PA

Burglary Case - Iowa City, Iowa

Lingle Murder Case

Marshall Square Bank Embezzlement

PAPERS:

1. "A Method for the Detection of Deception" — *American Journal of Police Science* (published by the Northwestern University Crime Detection Lab)
2. "The Canary Murder Case" — *American Journal of Police Science*

RESEARCH

1. Continued revision of methods in presenting deception tests
2. Physiological experiments with polygraph
   (a) Effect of amyl nitrate
   (b) Calibration of apparatus
3. Experiments with galvanometer in recording skin action currents and resistance — attempt to construct apparatus which will record above with ink or present apparatus (polygraph)
4. Experimentation with Dr. Muehlberger (toxicologist) to determine effect of scopolamine in the human subject. Value of the use of the drug as a "truth serum" and hypnotic — tests on two subjects with worthwhile and interesting results which warrant further study.

Nard was excited over his experiments with the galvanometer and truth serums, fascinating new approaches to uncovering the truth.

He had read about the Reverend Walter G. Summers, a New York priest and professor of psychology at Fordham University, who was experimenting with what he called a psychogalvanometer. The instrument, which was attached by electrodes to the hand, measured perspiration and the electric resistance of the skin, indicating emotional responses. Father Summers had already used it with some success on criminal suspects.

Scopolamine, or "twilight sleep", a partial anesthetic used frequently at that time to lessen the pain of childbirth, had the effect of blocking off the part of the brain that could think up a lie. Nard explained that telling a lie is a more complicated mental process than telling the truth. He used scopolamine, also sodium amytal, in some of his early cases, either alone or as a backup for the lie detector when a subject's responses were indecisive.

These experiments particularly interested Colonel Goddard, the director of the crime lab. He gave Nard his full support and encouragement in all his lie detection work, arranged for him to give talks and demonstrations at conferences and conventions of law enforcement officers, and often accompanied him on important out-of-town cases in which the lie detector was used. Since Nard did not have a medical degree, he was not qualified to administer drugs. Colonel Goddard, who did have an M.D., took full responsibility for the truth-serum experiments.

Nard had a story about a murder suspect who, under truth serum, rambled incoherently about his case until Nard shot the question, "What did you do with the gun?" "I threw it in the bushes", the man replied. This didn't sound right. Nard let the man ramble on a while longer, then fired the same question, "What did you do with the gun?" "I threw it in the river," replied the suspect.

Believing the experiment a fizzle, Nard decided to take a long shot. When the man was fully awake he informed him, "Well, George, we know all about you now. You told the whole story. You committed two murders. After one, you threw the gun in the bushes; after the other, you threw the gun in the river."

The man looked up aghast. "I told all that?"

"Yep."

Then the suspect gave up and confessed. He'd committed two crimes in addition to the one he'd been accused of. In trying to suppress that one, he'd unconsciously given himself away on the others.

Amazing as this case turned out to be, Nard seldom used any type of drug as a truth serum, except in very special cases, and then only with a doctor in attendance. However, he and some of his co-workers did try out various types of "truth detector" drugs on each other.

Nard had been working full-time at the lab only a few months when he had a telephone call from an old friend from Berkeley, Charlie Wilson. Charlie was at the depot on his way to New York and had a few hours to kill between trains. Could he come to the lab? Nard was delighted to see his old friend, who'd been with him in Troop 9 in the Boy Scouts and played cops and robbers with us on Dwight Way. When Charlie told him he had a job in New York in electronics, Nard urged him not to take it — to stay in Chicago. With Charlie's knack for mechanics and electrical gadgetry, he was just the man Nard needed to help with technicalities on the polygraph, and the galvanometer he wanted to add to it.

As Nard escorted him around the lab and introduced him to Kay, Colonel Goddard, Clarence Muehlberger, and all his co-workers, showed him the various types of apparatus used to solve crimes, and let him fire a few shots in the shooting range; Charlie was mightily intrigued. Colonel Goddard liked Charlie and was impressed by his technical know-how; Nard sold Goddard on the idea that he needed an assistant. And Charlie, rolypoly with dark, short-cropped hair, big brown eyes, affable, hot-tempered, never took that train to New York. Goddard hired him to work at the lab as research engineer and assistant in the department of psychology.

Ever the gracious host, Nard urged Charlie to stay with him and Kay until he found quarters of his own. And only weeks, or perhaps days, after Charlie moved out of their two-bedroom apartment, another freeloader moved in — me. I'd come to Chicago with a road company of a play, *Jonesy,* in which I'd acted on Broadway. The play turned out to be a hit, and instead of being in Chicago a few weeks as I'd expected, I was there for several months. Nard and Kay included me in their activities, took me to the crime lab, and let me in on all the excitement. Once, in the shooting range, they even had me fire a machine gun — a terrifying experience, like clutching a ferocious steel monster spitting bullets and struggling to escape.

Besides her job as secretary to Colonel Goddard, Kay was taking fencing lessons from a quaint little Frenchman. She was so enthusiastic over her newest hobby that she talked me into taking lessons too. But while I did learn to lunge, thrust, parry, and attack, having Monsieur's foil come at me, even though a button was on the tip, was unnerving. I soon gave it up. But Kay carried on until she became an expert. She had a remarkable talent for making a success of whatever she undertook. For example, wanting good clothes but lacking the money to buy them, she rented a sewing machine and took sewing lessons. Soon she had made an entire wardrobe, including professionally tailored suits and coats.

Often she'd arrive home from work early. Around five, Nard

would call and say, "I'll be home for dinner at 6:30 — and I'm bringing six people." Then Kay and I would go to the grocery store and bring home huge bags of food. Kay was an excellent cook, and Nard's bringing home half a dozen cronies for dinner didn't seem to throw her. Most were from the crime lab; some, such as Lance ("Bob") Robinson, from the Institute for Juvenile Research. The men would troop through the front door, removing their overcoats and plunking their guns on the hall table. Charlie, Nard's "body-guard" as we called him, was always along. The men congregated in the den to discuss the murders, rapes, and robberies they were working on and to listen to the police reports on the low-wavelength radio Charlie had installed. A deadpan voice would intone: "Squad 5 district 37 — at 241 Webster Street — a man is threatening to shoot his wife." Or: "robbery going on at such and such an address." At first it seemed gruesome to me, particularly the reports coming one after the other of domestic violence. But after a time I became used to it.

Nard was so engrossed in his work that I rarely saw him except around dinnertime — and then, usually with a crowd. He worked all day and often went out of town on cases.

During part of this time I worried about Nard, as I'd worried during his winter snowshoe trips in the high Sierra. I thought his life was in danger.

Jake Lingle, a police reporter, had been shot down in an underpass, it was believed by gangsters. Nard had worked on the case, and in the laboratory safe was the fatal bullet that had killed the reporter. One day as Nard was alone in his private office at the lab, two tough-looking gents sauntered in, shutting the door behind them. It was apparent they were there on business. When Nard asked politely, "What can I do for you gentlemen?", two pairs of eyes leveled at him menacingly. One of the men said, "We've come to make you an offer", the other, "We'll pay you $50,000 for the bullet that killed Jake Lingle." Nard's blood pressure must have shot up. He stalled, mumbling something about not having the combination to the safe. He'd have to see his assistant. "Wait here," he told the men. "I'll be right back." He walked rapidly out of his office and whispered to each of his co-workers, "Go back to the shooting range! Start firing machine guns! Hurry!"

Back in his own office he found the two strangers still waiting. Nonchalantly, he sat behind his desk and started to explain, "Sorry, gentlemen, I can't give you the bullet. It's evidence in a murder case, entrusted to us." The men started moving toward him ominously when suddenly the building shook and the windows rattled from the deafening roar of machine guns. Alarmed, the men glanced up. What was it? Gang war? The next thing Nard knew, they'd slunk out the door and were hightailing it out to their getaway car.

Grinning broadly, Nard rushed back to the shooting range and signaled the men to hold their fire.

Meanwhile, Kay was getting bored with her passive role as housewife and secretary. She felt Nard wasn't giving her enough attention. Instead of taking dictation, she wanted to dictate, to be an integral part of all that was happening. Mulling over the various techniques for identifying evidence, she finally decided on the field she'd like to specialize in — the examination of questioned documents. She began studying books on handwriting, types of paper, inks, variations in typewriters, and so forth, and before I left Chicago, she'd already mastered a considerable amount of knowledge. Later she studied with one of the top handwriting experts in the country and, in a short time, became amazingly proficient.

Years ahead of the women's liberation movement, Kay was capable and competitive. She refused to be held down or serve for long in a subservient position. An admirer of Amelia Earhart, Jacqueline Cochran, and other famous women flyers of that era, Kay also wanted to fly, both literally and figuratively. She wanted to break the bonds her sex imposed on her, to compete on equal terms in what was still a man's world.

Nard also believed in equality for women, although his beliefs were tempered by his streak of conventionality and the excesses of his sometimes wayward wife. Once, while she and Nard were traveling by train to the West Coast, Kay insisted on stopping off in Jackson Hole, Wyoming, where to everyone's astonishment she entered a rodeo — on horseback.

I've never known a more outrageously daring, complicated, or intriguing woman. Except in her occasional "moods", I liked her immensely. And I think she liked me. We somehow clicked.

And Nard, while often hurt or puzzled by her unpredictable behavior, was, deep down, incurably in love with her. He couldn't bear to be separated from her, even for a few days.

Charlie was another temperamental spirit, who could occasionally lose control. One night Nard and his gang went to Chinatown for dinner. Although the men rarely drank during the week, Saturday night was different, and on this particular Saturday Charlie had had a few too many. After dinner members of the group decided to try their luck at a nearby shooting gallery. When Charlie asked for a gun, the proprietor, aware of his condition, refused to give it to him. Then, to the consternation of everyone around, Charlie whipped out his own police revolver and blasted away at the make-believe ducks. There was a big to-do. I don't know whether Charlie was arrested, but nobody was hurt. And after that, you can believe, Charlie was mighty careful the way he handled firearms. In fact, he learned so much about them that he became one of the nation's leading civilian experts on firearm identification and explosives.

After I left Chicago, Nard and Kay also had a gun scare. They were sitting close to each other in the car when the gun in Nard's holster accidentally went off, tearing holes through both their clothes and grazing their thighs. But neither was really hurt.

In between my two long visits with Nard and Kay in Chicago, I'd lived in New York and had been very much in love with Bob Echols. Although even then I had some qualms. I was puzzled by his attitude toward what he called "the War Between the States" and his many references to "Damn Yankees." Was I, of New England ancestry, raised in California, one of these Damn Yankees he seemed to scorn? But, on my second visit to Chicago, he came out for a weekend to see me, and I was so thrilled to see him, all my apprehensions vanished. We decided to get married as soon as I returned to New York. That happened in early April. It was sad saying goodbye to Nard, Kay, Charlie, and all my new friends at the crime lab. I wished they could have come to my wedding. But there were too many crimes to be solved in Chicago. Both Nard and Charlie ran subjects on the lie detector every day. Soon they had so many cases that a third examiner had to be brought in. They were also far too busy for Nard to follow up on his experiments with the galvanometer. That telltale gadget would have to wait 'til later.

CHAPTER **6**

Interim, Back To The Books

During his first year at the crime lab, Nard worked on many cases — murders and armed robberies — that received front-page publicity.

The news stories usually referred to him as a lie detector expert associated with the Northwestern University Crime Detection Laboratory. Some called him the inventor of the lie detector, a frequent misstatement he tried to correct, and many alluded to him as a "Stanford graduate." The latter really messed up his blood pressure and respiration. It lay heavily on his conscience, and he was too embarrassed to admit it wasn't true. He had spent at least five years on (and off) the Stanford campus, yet he had never received his diploma.

So it happened that late in the spring of 1931, inspired by Chief Vollmer and his wife, who had recently returned to Berkeley, Nard decided to clear his conscience by returning to his old alma mater and getting his degree. Traveling by train, he and Kay visited father and Ormeida, our stepmother, in our studio in the Berkeley hills, where Nard and I spent our adolescence and where Nard first made headlines when one of his pet boa constrictors escaped.

In his log of that trip west he wrote: "Our home and garden are more beautiful than ever. What a land! Kay and I will never feel permanent, never satisfied till our home is here."

While at Stanford they bought a secondhand car for fifty dollars and made a number of trips to Berkeley to see father, boyhood friends, Chief Vollmer, and other crime experts. They also drove to San Francisco to meet Sanford Bates, director of

Federal Prisons, there to talk before the Commonwealth Club.
"Bates seems a fine man and was encouraging about the future
for university-trained men in the prison field," Nard wrote. Back
of the Stanford campus, Nard dug through Indian mounds with L.
D. Howard, then in medical school, later Uncle Sterling's assistant (the spot slated for Nard had he continued in medicine), and
sailed on the bay with "Cappy" Robinson, his friend Lance Robinson's father, who had been captain of a clipper ship. He and Kay
had many get-togethers, parties, and picnics with old college
friends still living in the vicinity. They also made two trips to
Oakland to persuade Jane De Armand, Charlie's pretty, blond,
nineteen-year-old girl friend, to come to Chicago.

Nard loved California. "This is paradise after the middle
west prairies," he wrote. "The hills look as if they mean business
poking up into the rolling banks of fog. The whole atmosphere is
clean, joyous, free. Faces smile, cheeks have color, society seems
organized. The depression hasn't creased faces or stiffened lips as
it has in Chicago. One lives here."

Another entry: "Last Friday in Palo Alto the thermometer
showed 109 degrees F in the early afternoon. Those poor devils in
Chicago! Charlie, I feel for you! It must be hell in that smoky,
stenchy, filthy atmosphere!"

About one of his classes, he noted: "I gave an argumentative
talk before the class in public speaking entitled 'The Jury System
Should be Abolished.' The criticism was that I stood with one
shoulder much lower than the other. God! Any chump could tell
me that! Why can't the prof help me with public speaking?"

In addition to public speaking, Nard was taking reading
research, biochemistry, and "a foolish course in elementary statistics required for a degree in psychology". His "last dash after
that artificial goal, that damned diploma." He'd been told by one
of his former professors that he must have set a record — more
hours signed up for, and more incompletes than any other
student.

Nard concluded his log with the story of "a student who
returned from World War I with only one quarter to go to finish
his B.A." He had been offered a fine position that would not be
open three months hence. He could not decide. He had a talk with
Ray Lyman Wilbur, the president of Stanford, then asked,

"Should I complete my university course or should I take this position?"

Wilbur asked three questions:

1. "Have you established some definite interest — have you discovered your goal?"

   "Yes."

2. "Have you learned how to obtain information about the things that you are so interested in which may lead you to that goal?"

   "Yes."

3. "Do you know how to apply that information to your problem?"

   "Yes."

"Well, that is all we can give you at this college. Don't waste your time finishing that last quarter. Take the position."

Nard commented, "Those are great words from a university president. If only he could put his theories into practice, the higher-educational system would rise from its dusty level to constructive heights!"

But despite Nard's gripes and his many extracurricular activities, in October 1931, he finally received his B. A. degree in psychology. Even then he lamented, "What a useless thing a sheepskin really is!"

But he needed that break in the sunshine. In Chicago, grim business awaited his attention.

CHAPTER 7

The Lie Detector Comes Of Age

After finishing that last quarter at Stanford and adventuring with Kay for a couple of weeks through the rugged beauty of the Northwest, Nard could hardly wait to get back to "hot, humid, filthy, stinking" Chicago.

For the tempo, the excitement, the challenge of that roaring, brawling metropolis was in his blood. A mecca for criminals, it was also a great industrial hub, a center of culture, and a wellspring of creativity. When visitors came, Nard was like the mayor, proudly showing off the sights of *his* city. He even stood up for its erratic climate — "If you don't like the weather, wait five minutes. It will change," he used to say.

He lived in Chicago at several different addresses, for some twenty years — eight of those working at the crime lab and the rest as head of his own firm. It was in Chicago that he and his lie detector won international recognition.

I've waited until this point to explain the exact workings of the lie detector and the techniques Nard and his associates devised because Nard was still refining them. But, in articles for the Journal of Police Science in the early 1930's, he explained this subject in his own words. In the balance of this chapter, I will quote some excerpts of Nard's articles, deleting some of the more technical aspects of the polygraph, which are described in books, such as *Lie Detection and Criminal Interrogation,* by John E. Reid and Fred E. Inbau, and in the operator's manual. And I hope Nard will forgive me for having continually referred to his instrument as a "lie detector," a name that has stuck since the early days in Berkeley when a newspaper reporter first called it that.

Nard wrote:

*LIE DETECTOR SOLVES MURDER   SUSPECT'S HIGH
BLOOD PRESSURE THWARTS LIE DETECTOR TEST
MACHINE SAYS SUSPECT LIES   SUSPECT SAYS
MACHINE LIES*

Such newspaper headlines and their accompanying stories
are taken up by paper pulp magazines with fantastic elabora-
tions. News stories on this order blossom forth when deception
tests are made at police stations, for reporters insist upon being
present, photographers attempt to snatch a picture or two, and
when the operator withholds results the journalist cheerfully
offers the public his own conception of them.

Laymen are led to believe that indicators jump in a defined
manner when a subject lies, or that a little red light flashes, or
that a bell rings. Certain so-called experts refer to their instruments as "lie detectors," and give the impression that they really
have such a device.

To begin with, there is no such thing as a "lie detector." There
are no instruments recording bodily changes, such as blood-
pressure, pulse, respiration, or galvanic reflex, that deserve the
name "lie detector" any more than a stethoscope, a clinical
thermometer, or a blood-count apparatus with a microscope can
be called an "appendicitis detector."

However, deception, guilt, or innocence can be diagnosed
from certain symptoms just as appendicitis, paranoia, or any
other physical or mental disorder can be diagnosed.

For instance, a patient is found to have a temperature of 102
degrees F., rigidity and pain in the appendix region, and a high
leucocyte count. From the combination of symptoms, the physician concludes that his patient is suffering with an infected
appendix. Or, in another case, the patient has delusions of perse-
cution, either systematized or ever changing fantasies, and various other symptoms that lead the psychiatrist to render a
diagnosis of schizophrenia or some other psychotic condition.

In detecting deception, the same general procedure is followed. Certain situations, or conditions, produce emotions that
are accompanied by bodily changes. The flushing of anger and the
paling with fear, for example, need no introduction. But to

discover, measure, and evaluate the less obvious bodily changes that accompany the emotions involved in deception requires just as much specialized care as the physician must exercise in making a complicated medical diagnosis.

Briefly, the apparatus for measuring and recording these bodily changes consists of three units — one, the cardiosphygmograph section makes a continuous recording of the individual's pulse rate, pulse wave amplitude, relative blood pressures and any changes in any of these. A second, the pneumograph section, makes a continuous recording of the individual's breathing movements, each inhalation and each exhalation action.(Later, a third was added, the galvanograph section which makes a continuous recording of the activities of the individual's sweat glands, and graphically illustrates any increase or decrease occurring in the individual's resistance. Some instruments today have additional sections and components for making additional recordings simultaneously of the individual being tested.)

The paper, perforated on its edges, is drawn by a sprocket feeder roll which is driven by a synchronous motor similar to that used in an electric clock ... A ninety-foot roll of paper supplies the recording chart, and the curves are recorded by means of combined lever arm and fountain pen ... The whole apparatus, or instrument, is contained in a carrying case measuring 16 × 8 × 9 inches. All accessories, the lead to the 110-volt outlet, signal magnet cord, blood pressure cuffs and tubing, and pneumograph are carried in a compartment above the mechanism compartment. The instrument is portable and always ready for immediate use. (Later, Nard had instruments built into desks.)

Much of the success of the blood-pressure technique in detection of deception and "guilt" has been attributed to the psychological effect such a test has on the suspect in bringing about confessions.

In a criminal case, self-protection is the dominant factor. The suspect has his reputation, his liberty, his life, or his money to lose if he is found guilty of an anti-social act, and so, if he is guilty of the act attributed to him, he will be dominated by fear. In a criminal case, the emotions of fear, anger, and rage enter as important factors.

A man, either innocent or guilty, accused of a criminal act, will have a considerable degree of apprehension. He may fear false accusation and conviction and may fear the treatment he believes is in store for him in the hands of the police. On the other hand, he may be angered by the accusation . . .

The customary steps are as follows: The suspect is brought into the laboratory, and immediately those in whose custody he had been are dismissed. In all probability, he has been "grilled" for some time before being subjected to the deception test and has come to view these officers with suspicion. On entering the laboratory, he is surrounded by a completely new environment and different personnel. The case is reviewed from the investigating officer's reports, after which the subject is briefly interviewed as follows:

"Well, young fellow, I can't see that they have much of a case against you. As far as I'm concerned, you have as much in your favor, if not more, than these officers have. Tell me now about this job you're supposed to have pulled." He is urged to tell his story. On completion, he is asked if he would submit to a little test — one in which his blood pressure, respiration, (and later galvanic skin responses) are recorded. "If you're innocent of this charge, I'm sure that we can determine as much in just a few minutes. I'm sorry this has happened. O.K.?"

In only a few cases out of thousands have suspects refused to submit to the test. If a man is innocent, he has nothing to fear and is glad to help in any way to prove his innocence. If he is guilty, he fears that a refusal to submit would indicate his guilt. Of course, if the suspect has retained an attorney, the latter may instruct his client to refuse. In case of a refusal, the suspect cannot be forced to submit to the test.

The subject is seated comfortably so he or she will not be facing the apparatus, the arm cuff is bound about the upper arm or leg, the pneumograph tube fastened about the chest or abdomen (depending on type of breathing), and the cuff system inflated to a point about halfway between the systolic and diastolic pressure. The pressure is maintained at this level throughout the test. Any changes in the individual's pulse or blood pressure will change the pressure of the system, deflecting the pen accordingly. The pressure may at the outset cause a little discomfort, but very few complain, and on instruction, most subjects will refrain from moving their arm. Any arm movement is recorded on the graph.

A record is obtained for twenty-five to thirty seconds to

ascertain the individual's normal fluctuations, heart activity, and respiration. Following this brief period of silence, a preamble is read:

"This instrument to which you are connected has been used for some years on criminal suspects, and so far has proved a very reliable means of detecting the truthfulness or deception of a person, and I'm sure we will not fail in your case. Now sit as quietly as possible, and answer my questions just yes or no. If you have any explanations to make, reserve them until the completion of the test."

During the reading of this preamble, a truthful person usually loses a certain amount of tension, relaxing and settling down to the task of answering the questions honestly. The deceptive suspect becomes more tense, however, as is indicated by an increase in general blood pressure and pulse rate.

Following this preliminary statement, two or three irrelevant questions are asked, such as: "Do you live in Chicago?" "Do you smoke?" "Are you married?" "Do you like to dance?" These allow the type of response in answering to be recorded. A truthful individual will seldom react in any marked degree to these questions. He regards them at their face value. A mentally defective (borderline) suspect, whether truthful or deceptive, may show but slight disturbance to these questions. However, a mentally alert, deceptive individual will construe them as being camouflaged questions regarding his crime. He may respond considerably more than the truthful person.

After these irrelevant questions are asked, direct questions pertaining to the supposed crime follow: "Did you dine with Jones Tuesday night?" "Did you return to Jones's apartment that night?" "Do you own a Savage forty-five?" "Did you shoot Jones?" These questions are asked in a quiet, monotonous voice. Time is allowed between questions for the bodily responses to occur and to return to equilibrium.

Usually, irrelevant questions are interposed among the relevant ones, or several such questions may be interposed in a group, thereby directing the suspect's attention away from his case for a moment. During this interrogation, the truthful person may respond slightly to questions, especially the first few, but these responses do not indicate great emotional stress.

The deceptive individual, on the other hand, becomes more

disturbed as the test progresses, the general blood-pressure curve rises, and the rapid fluctuations increase in intensity and frequency. The respiration becomes more rapid, or there is some other departure from the established norm, and in most cases the subject attempts to control his responses at periods following deception. The majority tend to shorten their inspiration and expiration and to breath slower. In consequence, there is a period of oxygen debit, and on the following questions, if pertaining to the crime, an occasional deep breath is taken. If the next questions are irrelevant to the crime, normal respiration is resumed, usually of greater magnitude than the preceding normal respiration.

The truthful suspect has no such fear, and is not prompted to control his emotional responses. His respiratory curve becomes more regular as the test progresses.

A single test of three to four minutes is sufficient to ascertain the deception or truthfulness of a suspect. If the suspect is determined to be deceptive, he is subjected to more questioning under a slightly different procedure. At the completion of the initial test, he may be shown his record, which is carefully explained to him. The examiner shows considerable concern over certain responses recorded thereon and asks the subject to explain his emotional stress. The more the deceptive person tries to explain, the more confused and entangled he becomes in his own story. For the second test, the deceptive person may be seated so that he can watch the excursions of the fluctuating pens; he is told to calm down and to see if he cannot run through a test without such disturbances as shown in the first record.

The deceptive individual now knows the instrument recorded his patterns of stress and that, if he is unable to control his responses during the second test, he surely will be shown to be deceptive. Due to his great apprehension, his fear is accentuated, and the second test may become more pronounced than the first. His added effort to control his responses during additional testing usually will cause greater disturbance, and his fear of the telltale pens will only tend to magnify each excursion as the relevant questions are asked.

On completion of this second test, or one or two subsequent tests, about 75% of the deceptive suspects make admissions. If a confession is not immediately obtained, a night spent in reflection may result in confession. The only "torture" involved in such a test is self-induced through fear of being caught, and that fear exists whether the person is being cross-examined in the usual way or on a polygraph instrument.

It is most important in this type of test that no methods shall be resorted to which will excite the suspect. All exciting factors must be eliminated, so that the responses will be due only to the case in question and not to physical or other psychological disturbances. The subject must be treated kindly and with respect at all times in order to induce relaxation and, as far as possible, to eliminate emotional tension. Best results are obtained when the examiner works on the theory that the subject is truthful and attempts to obtain as regular a curve as possible. The deceptive side of the situation will be well handled by the suspect himself.

Another type of case requires a slightly different testing procedure. In many criminal cases, there are details of which only the involved person is aware.

A burglar, busily engaged in opening a safe in a private home, was surprised by the sudden appearance of the owner. He jumped to a nearby window, and, in his clumsy effort to open it, he pulled down a curtain. Then, unable to escape, he started toward the door, shooting the owner as he ran. Fortunately, the bullet caused only a slight injury. The owner called the police immediately, and before morning five suspects were in custody. It is possible that all five men were professionals, and all knew they might be wanted for one job or another. Each man, in turn, was subjected to the deception test and questioned as follows:

1. Do you live in Balboa Park?
2. Do you live in the block the fire house is on?
3. Do you have a fire escape leading from your parlor window?
4. Do you have heavy curtains that might be easily pulled down on your windows?
5. Do you have a safe in your parlor?

No direct reference was made to the crime or to any crime. It happened that the five men held that night responded to none of the questions. They were unstable, but to no questions did they show a violent emotional response. Two days later, two more suspects were apprehended. One of these ran a clear record; the other responded significantly to each question which described the house robbed. Following the first test, another was given in which direct questions were asked. "Did you enter a private home on Elm Street?" "Did you attempt to open a safe?" "Did you shoot a man?" At the completion of the test, the suspect confessed. He was later identified by the man he shot.

The truthful suspects knew nothing of the burglarized house and in no way related the questions to any crime for which they may have been wanted. The guilty suspect immediately associated the questions with the house he had burglarized, and, in fear of being detected, responded clearly to each question.

CHAPTER 8

Murders Round The Clock

It was soon after Nard and Kay returned from their summer at Stanford that Jane De Armand, wide-eyed, pretty as a pinup, and unsuspecting, arrived in Chicago to marry Charlie Wilson. She'd met him the year before on a blind date.

Kay, Nard, and a few friends were at the wedding, held at a little chapel. There was a party of sorts afterward with hot dogs (or was it pizza?), beer, and much excited talk about specimens of handwriting, fingernail scrapings, gunpowder, explosions and corpses.

"I was scared to death," Jane admitted later. She was even more dismayed when Charlie, above the roar of gunfire, introduced her to his co-workers at the lab, pointing out a plaster cast of a human head and bloodstained garments to be examined and analyzed.

Fortunately, Jane was phlegmatic. For the first three years she stayed home, kept house, cooked for Charlie, sometimes also for Nard and Kay, and occasionally for the whole gang at the crime lab. "And afternoons I played bridge." Until the day Charlie and Nard decided the time had come to put Jane to work. But I'm jumping ahead of my story.

At the lab, Kay had been promoted from secretary to document examiner. Charlie not only assisted Nard with lie detector cases, but was becoming increasingly involved in firearm identification and other fields of criminal investigation. And, as Jane had suspected when she first arrived, everyone at the lab, in some way, at some time, was involved in that most frightening of all crimes — murder.

While Nard was still a consultant for the lab, before it was officially open, he was called in on an important murder case in Seattle, Washington.

It seems a young man, James Eugene Bassett, had been living with his parents on the East Coast and was on his way to the Philippines to take a position in Manila. On the way, he'd stopped in a suburb of Seattle to visit his sister. His sailing date was in ten days.

He'd driven across the continent in his own car, a fancy new roadster. This model was not yet on display in the west, and it had been much admired along his route. Bassett planned to take it with him to Manila, but at the last minute changed his mind and put an ad in the local paper offering it for sale.

A few days later a man came to the sister's home in answer to the ad. He seemed eager to buy but told Bassett he wanted his mother to see the car first. They arranged a meeting for the following day.

The next morning, telling his sister he'd return as soon as the deal was completed, Bassett drove off to meet the prospective buyer.

That was the last that was seen of James Bassett.

The next day Bassett's sister received a telegram: "I have sold my car and met a friend. Am going to Canada for a couple of days. Will return Friday — Jim."

Although he was not back by Friday, the sister thought nothing of it at that time. But when her brother failed to board the ship to Manila, she became alarmed and notified the police. She hadn't much to go on, but it was not like her brother to act this way. She couldn't believe he would have left the area, stayed away so long, and finally missed his ship, without telling her of his change of plans.

The next day, a businessman who'd read in the paper about Bassett's disappearance reported to police that he also had been visited by a prospective buyer in answer to an ad for the sale of *his* car. He described this stranger as menacing and thought he matched the description of the man Bassett had gone to meet.

Foul play now seemed certain. Descriptions of the car, of Barrett, and of the stranger were broadcast to police throughout the west, and a search began.

Two days later an alert police officer in Oakland stopped a car answering the description of Jim Bassett's Roadster. The driver of the car was Decasto Earl Mayer, a known criminal with many aliases who had served time in several penitentiaries. With Mayer was his sixty-three-year-old mother.

Jim Bassett's wrist watch, wallet, and other belongings were in the car.

Questioned at police headquarters, the couple claimed they had bought the car in a legitimate transaction. They produced the bill of sale, supposedly signed by Bassett.

When the police asked about Bassett's wrist watch and other property, the couple told them they'd found them in the car after the purchase. Thinking Bassett had sailed to the Philippines, they hadn't tried to return the articles, not knowing where to reach him.

The two suspects were then arrested and jailed in Oakland on a larceny charge. Each time they were questioned, they repeated that they had bought the car legally and knew nothing about Bassett's whereabouts. Meanwhile, police in Seattle, convinced that Bassett was dead, started a massive search for his body in an area where they knew Earl Mayer and his mother had been living. They dragged lakes and rivers, dug excavations, found no trace of the missing man.

The accused pair were then extradited to Seattle. They had retained a lawyer and continued to insist they were innocent. With the investigation at a dead end, the decision finally was made to call in Leonarde Keeler and his lie detector.

After being briefed by the prosecuting attorney, Nard set up his instrument, and over a period of several days, they questioned Mayer both on and off the polygraph.

At first Mayer treated the lie detector tests as a game. To find out where Bassett's body was, Nard asked, over and over, questions such as "Is it buried?" "Is it burned?" "Is it in a river?" "In a well?" To all these questions the answer was no, or else Mayer refused to speak, but in both cases the instrument registered no specific reactions.

Finally Nard used maps — first a map of the entire West Coast, then maps of California, Oregon, and Washington divided into numbered squares. Pointing to each square, Nard would ask, "Is Bassett's body in this area? In this? In this?" Even though Mayer refused to answer, Nard narrowed down the area to a specific region in Washington. He then divided maps of smaller areas into squares, and by this same technique eliminated all sections except one. The first strong reactions came when Nard pointed to a spot on this final map where Mayer had once made a down payment on a small house, a few miles from where he and his mother had recently lived. It was also close to a cemetery. (This house was later pinpointed as the site of the murder.) From then on, each time Nard asked about cemeteries or used the word *grave* or *slab,* the suspect became greatly agitated, thrashed about, and even pretended to faint.

Finally, with a map showing every grave in the cemetery, Nard intended to ask: "Is the body in this grave? In this one? In this?" But confronted with this particular map, Mayer refused to look at it. He seemed in a sort of stupor. Nard continued to question him. Then, abruptly, the prisoner roused from his lethargy, sprang up, and with terrific force smashed the lie detector. Two deputies grabbed him and returned him to his cell.

Nard was able to repair the damage to his instrument, and after letting Mayer rest for a day, he and the prosecuting attorney continued to question him. Finally Mayer asked if he would be given a fair trial. Assured that he would, he said he knew the lie detector had recorded the truth. He couldn't beat it. He admitted he had killed Jim Bassett. But he insisted that his mother had never done anything criminal except what he had made her do. Told that his mother would not be charged if Mayer led them to the grave where Jim Bassett was buried, Mayer agreed to comply.

It looked then as though the case was solved — as though the lie detector had trapped the criminal and located the body. Nard wired Kay in Chicago:

TOP BLEW OFF KETTLE THIS MORNING — PLENTY OF
EXCITEMENT — WE ACTUALLY OBTAINED CONFESSION
AND SOON WILL HAVE BODY.

Meantime, deputies searched for clues at the cemetery. Had Mayer buried Jim Bassett in another person's grave?

But that question was never to be completely answered. A shrewd new attorney Mayer had hired advised him to deny to authorities that he had confessed to the murder. Through the new attorney, a court order banning the use of the lie detector was obtained. The order also ruled that the prisoner was within his legal rights in refusing to testify when such a device was in operation. As Nard packed up to leave, he felt pretty good in one sense. The case had been a challenge; he'd developed new techniques of interrogation. But to be thwarted when the case was practically solved was a letdown.

After his return to Chicago, he learned that all efforts to find Jim Bassett's body had failed, and no direct evidence of homicide turned up. Therefore, it was not possible to charge Mayer and his mother with murder. Consequently, the prisoners were brought to trial on charges of grand larceny. Mayer was convicted as a habitual criminal and given a life term. His mother received five to ten years. And the body was never found.

Another important case Nard investigated for the crime lab concerned the murder of an attractive twenty-two-year-old girl, Rose Gendler. She lived in a small, midwestern city with her mother and stepfather, Mr. and Mrs. Jacob Mark.

Rose owned some real estate, including the house the family lived in. Her parents owned a local business. Rose worked only occasionally: it was during the Depression, and she felt that girls supporting their families should have the available jobs. But it happened that a few days before Christmas she was working at a store in a nearby town, helping out in the Christmas rush. On that particular night she left the store at 9:30 and started for home. Someone saw her take a streetcar. Later she was sighted on a commuter train. But she never got home.

Because Rose rarely stayed out late without telling her mother, Mrs. Mark became worried and called the police. No accident had been reported, and the police assured the mother her daughter probably would arrive home any minute. After several hours, however, when Rose still had not returned, police officers arrived at the house and began a search. At 4:00 a.m., they found a note tacked to the back door demanding two thousand dollars ransom. The police and Rose's parents were puzzled — after all, the family was not wealthy. Why should anyone kidnap Rose for a ransom?

Then, at 8:30 the next morning, Rose was found — dead. Her body in a gunny sack, lay under a bridge on the surface of a frozen river not far away. Apparently the killer had dropped the body from the bridge, expecting it to break through the ice and disappear until the spring thaw. The body had sustained many wounds, including deep gashes on the head. Because the girl's underwear had been torn, the police at first believed Rose had been sexually attacked, but according to the medical report, this was not true.

Family members including the mother, stepfather, and stepbrothers were questioned by the police. They also questioned Mr. and Mrs. Meyer and their son, Maurice, close friends of the Marks who lived nearby. But the officers could not unearth anything that might lead to the perpetrator of the crime. Rose had few men friends. She had lived a sheltered life. The Meyers tried to help, and Maurice Meyer, their twenty-five-year-old son, who was half-owner of a laundry, described the girl's fine character and reputation.

The police of several nearby communities undertook a joint search for the murderer but no clues turned up. Finally, the investigators decided to call in Nard to examine the stepfather, two stepbrothers, Mr. Meyer, and his son Maurice on the lie detector.

Rose's parents were greatly disturbed. They didn't want their friends the Meyers to be subjected to this sort of indignity. But the officers insisted, and for two days Nard questioned each member of the group on the polygraph.

Very suddenly, Maurice Meyer disappeared. Suspicious, the police started checking up on Maurice, who had claimed to be asleep in bed at the time Rose was murdered. They collected dust from the trunk of Maurice's car and sweepings from his laundry and compared them with the dirt and dust on the gunny sack in which the body had been discovered.

The investigators learned that on the night of the crime, Rose had telephoned Maurice from the store where she worked and asked him to meet her. The micrographer at the crime lab had discovered that the dust taken from Maurice's car and laundry matched particles on the gunny sack.

Believing they had found the suspect, the officers were about to file a murder charge against Maurice Meyer, when suddenly he appeared voluntarily at police headquarters. He'd been in Los Angeles, he said, and had come back to tell everything he knew.

He admitted he'd called Rose the night she died and said, "If I'd met her, she wouldn't have died." One of the investigating officers then informed him, "We know you had her body in that sack in your car the night she disappeared. We have the facts. If you know what's good for you, you'll tell us everything." Greatly agitated, Maurice insisted he hadn't killed Rose. She'd had a fall—hurt herself. He was frightened and threw her body off the bridge because he knew no one would believe him if he said he hadn't killed her. Then he'd been so panicky that he decided to write a ransom note so that no one would suspect him.

The police did not believe his story, and Maurice Meyer was brought to trial.

To establish a motive, the prosecutor reiterated that the girl's underwear had been torn, that Maurice Meyer had tried to seduce her but had been repulsed. In a frenzy of frustration and rage, he'd struck out at her and knocked her unconscious. Then afraid he'd be found out, he killed her.

The defendant was found guilty.

In Nard's case file I found the questions that he had asked Maurice Meyer. "Is your name Maurice Meyer?" "Do you live in Rock Island?" "Do you know who killed Rose Gendler?" "Did you have breakfast this morning?" "Did you have anything to do with Rose Gendler's death?" "Do you know where the gunny sack came from that was used to hide the body?" "Did you have any connection with the killing of Rose Gendler?"

In the second test, when Nard asked him the names of approximately twenty people who might have had some part in the killing, Meyer's blood pressure rose slowly, his respiration indicating suppression through the point where his own name was asked. After that, his blood pressure dropped and his respiration indicated definite relief.

Nard repeated this test twice to verify the reaction. Then he asked Meyer a group of questions to determine what type of car he had used to transport the girl. Meyer responded to "touring car," the type of car he owned.

Following this test Nard again questioned Meyer, and although he gave no outward appearance of nervousness or guilt, the polygraph records definitely implicated him in the death of Rose.

But, as I have stressed before, polygraph tests alone do not convict suspects. There must be corroborating evidence, as there was in this case.

Some of Nard's cases were bizarre. Take, for instance, the case of Clara Condon. The attractive thirty-five-year-old wife of Stephen Condon, a local merchant, she consulted a seer who told fortunes with illustrated cards. According to the mystic, the first three cards Clara drew foretold that Clara's husband would be murdered. Strangely stimulated by this grim prediction, Clara hurried home to tell Stephen and a few neighbors.

Two weeks later, with her nine-year-old son, Peter, she returned home to find Stephen on the kitchen floor — dead. His pockets had been turned inside out; his empty wallet was on the floor.

Clara called the police. The officer who arrived believed Stephen had been murdered by a burglar, until he noticed that the dead man had been shot twice — once on each side of the head. Little Peter then spoke up: "My father's death was predicted by a fortune teller." Asked where he had heard this, the boy replied, "My mother told my father. She said in a little while she'd be a widow."

News of the "death-card slaying" got around. Clients wanting to have their cards read besieged the fortune teller. A newspaper reporter claimed, after having her cards read, that the fortune teller's predictions were vague and could apply to anyone.

After Stephen's funeral, which was mobbed by curiosity seekers, the police rounded up several of Clara's men friends. They also looked into Stephen Condon's insurance and learned that Clara's brother, once an insurance agent, had written a $5,000 policy on his brother-in-law's life. Later, Clara had changed it to a $7,000 policy paying double indemnity for a death by violence or accident.

Nard, by then part of the investigation, tested the various principals on the lie detector. As a result of the police work and the polygrams of Clara Condon and her brother, all those involved in the plot, including one of Clara's men friends, were tried and received life sentences. Clara was given fourteen years for her part in the conspiracy that resulted in her husband's death.

CHAPTER 9

Embezzlers Beware!

In addition to sensational murders, Nard often worked for banks, savings and loan associations, insurance companies, and other business organizations with large numbers of employees who handled or had access to other peoples' money. During his first year at the crime lab, he wrote the following report:

In conducting various bank examinations, we have found considerable petty embezzlement irregularities. In one bank, a drug addict and two men with previous police records were discovered.

I have suggested to several banks that all new employees might be examined with the aid of the polygraph and other available character tests in order that the officials might employ with 'open eyes.' After a few successful bank cases have been concluded, I believe it will be opportune to suggest to bank officials that the Scientific Crime Detection Laboratory be retained for given periods at a given fee to examine employees in cases of embezzlement or other irregularities in order to determine guilt or innocence of individuals. All new employees might well be submitted to the same type of test to ascertain their integrity.

In March, 1934, Nard reported this:

In the past three and a half years at this laboratory, the deception test has been used in 405 criminal and personnel cases, in which 2,809 persons were tested. The personnel cases involved criminality in some instances and were conducted in 45 banks and eight or nine other institutions.

It has been found in the banks examined that 10% to 23% of the

personnel have taken some money. In only one bank have we
obtained confessions of theft from less than 10% of the employees,
although in some cases, confessions of thefts amounting to
thousands of dollars have been obtained. The usual thefts are of
small amounts.

Six or seven banks have each candidate (job applicant) tested
before accepting him (or her) for employment. At one bank we
found (by confession to verify test results), only one suitable
candidate out of 12 examined. In two recent cases confessions were
obtained from bank employees to the effect they intended and had
planned to steal large amounts of money. One had planned to take
a hundred thousand dollars; the other an even larger amount.

In one bank, of 26 employees tested, Nard obtained six
confessions of theft. One employee responded in the test to having
taken $1,490 that was reported missing but only admitted taking
amounts up to $500. A candidate for a bank job confessed to
having taken $3,500 from the bank where he was previously
employed, and the vice-president and cashier confessed to having
played the stock market (in 1929) with bank money. Nard found
that when top executives appropriate funds for their own use,
there's apt to be dishonesty all through the organization.

Embezzlement was not all that Nard uncovered during his
examinations of bank employees. In an unusual case, one employee who tested poorly finally admitted, after being shown his
graph and questioned off the polygraph, that he had stolen money
but *not* from the bank. He and several of his co-workers had
collected funds for a charity by standing on the street with a tin
can for donations. It was from this can that he'd stolen money.
Fascinated, Nard asked that all the other employees who had
worked on this charitable campaign be given polygraph tests.
Regarding the integrity of the human race, the results were
disheartening: of some ten participants, all but one admitted
stealing the charity money. Nard explained: "They didn't think
anyone could possibly find out."

Often insurance companies called Nard into bank cases. One
involved the theft of a safe-deposit box allegedly containing
$26,000 in cash. The bank, Northwest Security National Bank, of
Sioux Falls, South Dakota, had insured its vaults against such
losses. In this case, Nard learned from bank executives and the
insurance adjuster, the victim of the theft was Dr. O. V. Opheim,

a physician in his sixties who visited the bank almost every day. The tellers thought him eccentric and suspected he was stashing currency in his safety box to avoid paying income tax.

First the investigators inspected one vault, reached through a heavy door with a time clock. At the far end were the bank safes, and along the walls the safe-deposit boxes. Outside the vault door were the custodian's desk and three booths where customers could go through their boxes in privacy. Two keys were needed to open the safety boxes — a master key kept by the vault custodian and the customer's key.

When leasing a box, a customer received two keys. The bank did not have duplicates, so if the customer lost both keys, the box had to be drilled open, the lock changed, and new keys supplied. To get into their safety box customers had to write their name, box number, and the time on a slip of paper for the custodian to verify and sign. Then the customer was supposed to accompany the custodian into the vault where the custodian would put the master key in the lock before the customer could open the box with his key. But often these procedures were lax. Customers sometimes left their keys in the lock while they went into one of the booths or were careless in other ways.

In addition to the custodian's set of master keys, four other sets were kept by three vice-presidents and an assistant cashier. The head janitor did all the servicing and repair work on the safety boxes and had free access to the vault and to the custodian's set of master keys.

Dr. Opheim who leased the missing box checked to see that he had both his keys. He did. But there was some suspicion regarding him. The custodian, a young woman, told the insurance adjuster that he had once taken her master keys without her permission. Later she'd seen him in the vault with the keys, wearing an overcoat.

Before Nard started the tests, the insurance adjuster explained that, first they wanted to know if the doctor has actually sustained a loss, and, if so, how much. After hearing all the details, Nard set up his portable polygraph in the director's room of the bank. It was decided to test the doctor and 26 subjects who had access to the vault.

Over a four-day period, in the presence of the bank president and the insurance adjusters, Nard interrogated bank officials, the head janitor, vault custodian, the doctor whose safety box had vanished, and all the rest. The insurance adjusters had called the bank inefficient, but Nard was amazed at the apparent honesty of the employees. Not one of the subjects showed deceptive reactions on the polygraph.

But one had not yet been tested, Charles Falck, the assistant cashier. After attaching this last subject to the instrument and asking a few irrelevant questions, Nard realized the man was extremely nervous. "Innocent people often show signs of nervousness," he explained to the officials watching. But when Nard asked the subject if he'd taken the doctor's safety box, his reaction was significant.

Besides money, there had been stocks, bonds, a passport, citizenship papers, and other items in the box. In a "peak of tension test," Nard read the names of these items. The assistant cashier reacted specifically to "passport" and "citizenship papers." After several more tests, aware that his emotions were revealing his guilt, the man admitted that he had taken the doctor's safety box and all the contents. The money, he said, was hidden behind a panel in his bathroom closet at home. He'd destroyed the papers and had cut up the metal box with a large pair of tin shears and strewn the pieces along a section of the highway.

Following this dramatic confession, Mr. Falck took the insurance adjuster, bank officers, and Nard to his home where he removed a panel from the linen closet and took out several large envelopes stuffed with bills. The bank president counted them — $25,520!

The suspect then told how he'd done it. He had a young son who'd been given a modeling set for Christmas. Watching the boy make little figures out of the clay had given him an idea. He started carrying a ball of the clay — about the size of a marble — around in his pocket.

He'd watch customers go into the vault to take out their safety boxes. When one carelessly left his or her key in the compartment door while going through papers in a booth, Falck took the key out of the slot and pressed it into this modeling clay, stuck the clay in his pocket, inserted the key back into the lock, and went home. There he had a set of blank keys and a grinding machine, and he'd make a duplicate key.

The investigators found he had keys to a number of the boxes. When he had the opportunity, with no one around, he'd open the boxes with his master keys and his duplicates of the customers' keys. He'd known about the large sums of money in the doctor's safety box and several times had opened the box and looked into it. Then, one day at closing time, he'd taken it out, hidden it under his overcoat, and left the bank.

After this confession, Nard still was not satisfied. He took the group to his hotel room where he gave the suspect another polygraph test. After this second test, Nard believed the assistant cashier was still withholding the entire truth and urged him to tell all. Finally, the embarrassed bank official decided to relieve his conscience. He'd been stealing since childhood, he admitted. He'd taken $80 from an office at college, $300 from another bank where he'd worked, and he'd stolen various small amounts from this bank.

In the following days, many of the thefts admitted by the suspect were verified. Pieces of the metal safety box that he'd cut

Nard examines Dorothy Steffensen (secretary posing as "subject") on the Keeler Polygraph, still in use.

up were found where he said he'd dropped them. And several customers he mentioned told the investigators they had found small sums missing from their boxes, but thought they had simply been careless.

A year later the president of the bank wrote Nard to say that a polygraph was to be purchased for their general counsel's office. No further trouble had arisen at the bank since Nard had been out there for the previous spring, he said. They'd had several scares when depositors came in to check their boxes, but no losses were reported, so Nard could feel he'd cleaned up the job while he was there. They now had a uniformed guard, and it would take almost an act of Congress to get into their vault.

In another bank case, an employee undergoing a routine polygraph test admitted stealing several thousand dollars. Asked how he had spent the money, he smiled faintly. "Well, I guess you'll think I'm crazy," he said, "but, I didn't use the money for myself. During the Depression, several of my friends were unemployed and in desperate circumstances. They had families to support. I conceived the idea of telling them that I had been employed as an undercover agent for a chain store and that I was being paid by the company to employ seven or eight individuals to serve as secret inspectors.

"All these friends of mine spent their evenings visiting stores of the chain, noticing the neatness of the employees, the arrangement of merchandise on the counters and in the show cases, noting promptness of service and other details. Later, they turned in written reports to me, and I paid them out of the cash I had stolen from the bank."

At the end of the interview, the young man laughed: "Well, when my friends hear about this, they'll certainly feel foolish for making all those fake investigations."

Nard also tested a number of young job applicants who admitted after the test that, while serving as altar boys in churches, they had helped themselves to money in the offering plates.

Then there was the teller who, a bank officer assured Nard, was 100 percent honest. Every day for years he'd balanced his account to the penny. But Nard, skeptical, thought he'd been stealing, then shortchanging his customers. The teller's polygram and subsequent confession proved Nard's suspicions correct.

But despite the prevalence of petty thefts, Nard emphasized that, while banks have what they call "counter" losses, the amounts stolen by employees are usually insignificant compared to the vast sums taken in and paid out by the tellers and do not affect the safety of depositors' funds. Generally, he recommended keeping employees who confessed to small thefts of money or merchandise, with the understanding that in six months they would be tested a second time. Once caught stealing, few would endure the embarrassment of being caught, again.

By this means, many Chicago banks, stores, and other organizations cut losses from embezzlement and thievery dramatically. The lie detector not only helped to catch criminals, it also prevented crime while saving the jobs of those whose pilferage was minor.

CHAPTER 10

More Cases From Extortion To Horse Stealing

Murders, burglaries, and bank embezzlements far from exhausted the repertoire of cases Nard took on with his lie detector.

He examined scores of employees of chain and department stores to find out who was stealing money or merchandise. In one firm he screened employees to determine who was giving information to a competitor. He ran jockeys, stable hands, and other employees of a racetrack to spot the culprit who was doping horses.

Many cases dealt with anonymous messages — extortion notes, poison pen and threatening letters, indecent and threatening telephone calls, and anonymous telegrams. Becoming a full-fledged document examiner at the crime lab when the former examiner left, Kay collaborated with Nard on a number of such cases. "Threatening notes are usually written by cranks or extortionists and often sent to people who have had their names or pictures in the paper," Nard explained. As an example, he'd cite the case of a man who sent extortion notes to four brides from socially prominent families. The notes threatened death if a certain sum was not forthcoming. Kay proved that all the notes were written on the same typewriter. The police then had the father of one of the brides write to the extortioner that the package of money would be left in an apartment house areaway. When the extortioner arrived to pick up the package, policemen hidden nearby seized him.

I have no record that Nard worked on this case. The extortionist was caught so quickly, his services were probably not needed. But the following shows how he and Kay collaborated on cases involving handwriting.

A young man, James J. McCormack, employed by Pan American Airways in Chicago, was accused of sending an anonymous telegram to the corporation president in New York, stating that something was wrong with one of the managers of the Chicago office, because that manager had fired so many men from his department. The telegram was signed "Thomas." No one named Thomas worked in the office.

Three handwriting experts who examined the specimens of writing involved (hand printing) judged that the telegram had been sent by McCormack, since his writing, also hand printing, bore a striking similarity to the writing on the telegram blank. But there were still some doubts, McCormack was sent to the crime lab for a polygraph test. On two different days, Nard administered a total of seven tests and found no significant response indicating guilt.

Meanwhile, McCormack had been fired from his job and was determined to clear up this case against him.

Nard then had Kay examine the handwriting on the telegram blank. Kay reported that both in number and individuality the differences between McCormack's handwriting and the writing on the telegram blank far exceeded the similarities. The differences, she stated, were not of the sort usually produced by an attempt at disguise; they were too subtle and consistent. She said that a person can't repeatedly, consistently, and rapidly suppress his natural, habitual forms and substitute others. Although it's not impossible, it's improbable.

Comparing the writing on the telegram blank to other specimens of McCormack's handwriting; notations he jotted down before the date of the anonymous telegram (a hotel reservation, birthday message, and so on) and samples he wrote at the crime lab; Kay concluded her report: "In the opinion of the examiner, the questioned handwriting and specimens of McCormack's writing were not written by the same person."

Despite the concurring polygraph and handwriting reports from Nard and Kay, the head of the Chicago office where McCormack had worked was not completely satisfied. He consulted one

Nard and Kay working together on case.

more expert in New York, considered the greatest handwriting authority in the country. This expert's report agreed almost point for point with Kay's. And, at last, officials of this corporation were convinced that James McCormack had not written the anonymous telegram.

Some of Nard's cases involved arson. "Frequently arson is a psychological problem," he explained. "Although not always. While there are true pyromaniacs (persons who get a sexual thrill out of setting fires), there are other individuals who start fires to collect insurance or for other motives such as revenge."

Two questions Nard generally asked suspected arsonists were: "Do you know who set the fire?" and "Did you set the fire?" He also had to look out for rationalizations: the suspect may have "fixed" electric wires the week before and considered that not he but the wire set the fire.

To test for pyromania, Nard sometimes flashed a cigarette lighter so the suspect could see it out of the corner of his eye, or he'd throw a lighted match into the wastebasket. Once, while examining an arson suspect, Nard stepped out of the examination room between tests and watched the man for a few minutes through a mirror arrangement. Sitting alone, the suspect set a piece of paper on fire, waved it in the air, his eyes gleaming wildly, and kept repeating, "Oh, see the pretty flames! See the pretty flames!" To his polygraph students, Nard would explain, "Showing a pyromaniac an open flame will often bring forth a confession."

Then there were cases involving malingerers. An insurance adjuster brought Nard a man suspected of faking blindness in one eye. The accused man had passed all the tests given by doctors; when one doctor jabbed a finger at his supposedly blind eye, for instance, it hadn't shown the slightest blink or tremor.

After his usual introductory spiel, Nard placed a patch over the subject's good eye, leaving the "sightless" eye exposed. Then he attached the subject to the polygraph, turned on the chart drive system, and, after recording the subject's normal reactions, had Charlie Wilson, who assisted him, hold up a picture of a country village. The subject's blood pressure and breathing registered little fluctuation on the graph. Charlie then showed a pastoral scene, without drawing a reaction, then a sunset, a seascape, a winding road; still with no response.

Then, quickly, Charlie flashed a pornographic picture before the "sightless" eye. Outwardly the subject showed complete calm, no reaction whatsoever — but the pens of the polygraph went wild.

Nard and Charlie repeated this test, obtaining the same giveaway reaction. The subject's claim for loss of sight was not paid.

Several years later, after Nard had left the crime lab and had his own business, T. P. Sullivan of the Illinois Bureau of Investigation, called him to leave at once for Stateville Penitentiary on a matter of life or death. Three men had tried to escape — Peter, Joseph, and Patrick. They had rushed to a wall with a ladder they had made, but were caught before they could climb over. All the tower guards had been drugged and were seriously ill. To find out what drug had been used to poison them, Nard ran Pete, Joe, and Pat on the polygraph. First, he read each of them a list of names of suspected accomplices. Among them was a convict serving a life term for murder who helped in the kitchen. King was his first name.

Each of the three men tested responded specifically to "King." Nard then read a list of drugs to each man:

1. Digitalis
2. Aspirin
3. Belladonna
4. Strophanthus
5. Scopolamine
6. Hyoscine
7. Stramonium
8. Atropine
9. Nicotine flower
10. Morphine
11. Chloral
12. Bromides
13. Luminol

Each prisoner responded specifically to hyoscine. These tests then showed that King had placed hyoscine in pitchers of tea and coffee destined for the tower guards. The guards were treated accordingly, and soon recovered.

Another early case that particularly pleased Nard occurred in Black Creek, Wisconsin. Nard described it in his own words:

A small bank was robbed in the afternoon, at about three o'clock. It so happened that two men, soliciting for a collection agency in Chicago, went into that district, identified themselves at the bank, and obtained two delinquent accounts. They left the bank and started toward the next town on their list.

At exactly three o'clock that afternoon the bank was robbed. A woman cashier said that she could identify the two men from the collection agency as the robbers. They were arrested in Durand, a town some distance away.

Having been en route at the time of the robbery, the men had a weak alibi. The woman cashier, three men in the bank, and a filling station attendant from across the street who saw the robbers, testified they could identify the two collectors as the robbers.

The defending lawyer knew of no way to save his clients from a verdict of guilty. Finally he decided to have them tested on the polygraph and have the results, if favorable, introduced into court.

We examined the two men and each gave an absolutely clear

record. In fact, one of the men gave his biggest response on the
machine to the question: "Did you graduate from college?" [Which
must have rung a bell with Nard.]

We went to court, told how the machine worked and the experience we had with it. The judge finally asked the prosecutor if he
had any objection to its (the polygraph records) admission before
the jury. The prosecutor objected. He said: "You are usurping the
right of the jury. The law provides that the jury be selected to
determine whether or not these men are guilty and cannot have
anyone come from the City of Chicago with a little black box and
tell the jury what verdit to reach." The judge ruled the testimony
out because of his unfamiliarity with the methods employed.

However, two days before the case went into the hands of the
jury, two men were arrested in another mid-western city, and
during their confessions to other bank robberies, they admitted
they had held up the Black Creek bank, which the two collection
agents had visited just before the hold-up.

The trial of the two collection agents was suspended for a short
time, and the witnesses rushed to the other city to see the men who
had confessed to the robbery. The woman cashier said: "My gracious, yes. Those are the men." One of the real bank robbers then
said to her: "How do you know? You were lying on your stomach in
that bank crying like a baby when I robbed it and you didn't see me
nor anyone else."

It would be possible to recount case after case along similar lines.

As I have already mentioned, the polygraph was not generally accepted in court, but there were exceptions. Nard kept a
transcript of another of his court appearances. Undated and
unsigned, it appears to be the trial of a man accused of stealing a
race horse. After being questioned in detail on his qualifications
as an expert, Nard was asked:

Q. Have you used the polygraph in court?
A. On many occasions, by stipulation between the defense
and prosecution, and in other cases in which we had confessions
admitted as evidence.

Defense Attorney. Accepted by the defense as an expert
witness.

Proscuting Attorney. On January 15, 1939, did you receive a communication from anyone in this city to come to Tulsa?

A. I received a communication from Inspector Houghton, asking me to come here to make an examination of a horse thief.

Q. Did he say who that horse thief was?
A. Yes, Lou Rubens of Joliet, Illinois.

Q. Do you see Lou Rubens here?
A. Yes, this gentleman with the blue shirt on *(indicating the defendant)*.

Q. Did you give a polygraph examination to Lou Rubens?
A. I did.

Q. Did you give this examination with his consent?
A. I did.

Q. Did he ask for the examination?
A. I understand that he asked for it and he asked if he could have all the evidence that came up.

Q. And you gave him a complete test?
A. Yes, five tests.

Q. Will you describe what happened?
A. For half an hour I talked to Mr. Rubens and explained the mechanism and the purpose of the test and asked if he wanted to submit to the lie detector, and he said, "Sure, I'll take it." I put the blood-pressure strap on and proceeded to take the test, and ran a normal, for some four or five minutes.

Q. What is a normal?
A. I wanted to see if he had any heart trouble or how excited he was. Although he was apparently calm, his pulse frequency was about 120. Normal is 70-75.

Q. Was he thinking about this case?
A. I imagine he was. After running normal three or four minutes, and after several blood pressure tests, I asked him two irrelevant questions: "Is your name Rubens?" "Do you live in Tulsa? Then I asked, "Do you know who stole the horse?" For the next 15 seconds he took very short breaths. It was his conscious effort to cover up; he was trying to control the changes in blood

pressure and breathing so they would not be recorded on the machine. The next question was irrelevant — "Are you married?" After answering, Mr. Rubens took four or five very deep breaths, and when he came back to his norm I asked, "Did you steal the horse?" and he had a change in responses again. I repeated the questions and went into various details until we completed the test.

Q. Did you find out whether he was a psychopathic type?

A. I found he was a normal individual in many respects, but he had a complex on horses. After an hour and a half of questioning off the machine, he broke down and admitted that he was in Tulsa at the time and that he had stolen the horse, going into detail as to the occurrence of that night.

Q. And he told you at that time he stole Jeepers Creepers?

A. I didn't know the name of the horse at the time.

Defense Attorney. I move that all of the testimony concerning the alleged confession be stricken because I should have objected to it at the outset. Before a confession is admissible, there must be a showing that it was procured without any promise of immunity or without threats or intimidation. That it was procured freely, there is not any evidence in this record to show.

The Court. Objection overruled, for the reason that the testimony is that which the defendant personally requested. He asked for this examination to prove his innocence.

There was more, but the transcript did not reveal the outcome of this particular case.

CHAPTER 11

Acclaim And Fame

Early in 1933, at a banquet at the LaSalle Hotel, Nard, then only twenty-nine, received a great honor; the Distinguished Service Award of the Junior Association of Commerce, for the most outstanding civic contribution to Chicago for the year 1932 by a young man between the ages of twenty-one and thirty-five.

In introducing Nard, the spokesman for the award committee described the committee's extensive search among eligible men from every field of activity. He reviewed Nard's life and his work under Chief Vollmer and Dr. Herman Adler at the Institute for Juvenile Research, then told of the invention of the Keeler Polygraph, how Nard had steadily improved it, and finally how well it had worked at the Northwestern Scientific Crime Detection Laboratory during 1932. In the first eleven months of that year, 87 cases had been handled, with some 626 perons tested on the instrument. The speaker pointed out, fifty-four confessions had resulted. After running guilty tests, only eight individuals had refused to confess, most on advice of counsel.

"The steadily growing number of cases on which Mr. Keeler is called, many of them in points distant from Chicago, shows that his work is winning increasing recognition," the spokesman continued. "In fact, it is no exaggeration to say that the laboratory is fast becoming a second Scotland Yard ... The American Prison Congress passed a resolution at its national conference last October endorsing the work of the crime detection laboratory, of which Mr. Keeler's activities constitute a prominent part. The international Association of Chiefs of Police also expressed its approval in a special resolution."

The speaker concluded: "Mr. Keeler's attitude is that of the true scientist. He makes no claims of infallibility, either for his machine or his tests, and he is constantly working for improvement . . . The field in which he is doing research work is a new one, with but a few guideposts, and his contributions will undoubtedly prove highly valuable in bringing about needed reforms in our methods of dealing with criminals and crime."

After this introduction, Nard gave a talk and demonstrated his machine.

News of the award appeared in newspapers coast to coast, and accolades arrived from family, friends, and business associates. In a letter dated February 7, 1933, Sanford Bates, director of the Federal Bureau of Prisons, wrote, congratulating Nard on his important achievement.

Father, too, was extremely proud of his son. Since leaving the Berkeley Chamber of Commerce, father had written two series of radio dramas broadcast weekly over a period of several years. But after the second series ended, father's financial problems resumed. From then until father's death, Nard helped out with a monthly check; "to pay in part for all that you have done for me."

Nard did feel that his Distinguished Service Award was not only for himself, but also for his father, who had instilled in him the importance of honesty and subsidized his original invention; for Chief Vollmer and those he'd worked with in the early days in California; and for all his associates at the crime lab.

As Colonel Goddard stated in an article reprinted in the September 1976 issue of the *Journal of the American Polygraph Association:* "Together we had sold a skeptical world the idea that there was something in the lie detector, something in a truth serum, and together we had mingled our blood and sweat in building up the first scientific crime detection laboratory in America, the first training class in police laboratory methods, and in developing the first truly scientific police journal to appear in the United States. That was the *American Journal of Police Sciences,* of which I was editor-in-chief from its establishment in 1930 to 1932 when it was combined with the *Journal of Criminal Law.*"

Nard, Kay, Charlie, and most of the other staff members wrote articles for the *American Journal.* They also taught classes in the four-week courses on "Methods of Scientific Crime Detection," which brought police officers and criminologists from all over the country. Among the subjects Nard taught, either alone or in collaboration were: Elementary Physiology, Elementary Psychology, Demonstration of Methods for Detecting Deception, Uses of Ultra-violet Rays, Laboratory Demonstrations of Moulage Methods (with Prof. Muehlberger), and Demonstration of Truth Serum (with Charlie). Kay taught classes with Mr. Walter in handwriting and typewriting identification.

Before buying a Keeler Polygraph, taking the four-week course was a precondition. The Western Electro Mechanical Company, Inc., in Oakland, still manufactured the machines and sold them only to law enforcement officers, criminologists, and other qualified persons in allied fields. To Nard this training was critical: "The inexperienced operator," he wrote, "cannot diagnose deception with a polygraph any more than he can diagnose a cardiac murmur with a stethoscope."

The night of the award banquet brought Nard more than fame. It was also the beginning of stress.

From now on, he would no longer be the boy wonder or the "youthful" Leonarde Keeler. He was recognized now as the authority in his field. He'd have friends galore — many who loved him for his charm, his gift of storytelling and way with people. Others would want something or would envy his popularity. He'd have enemies, too, trying to discredit him.

To Kay, Nard's recognition served as a challenge to work harder than ever on her document cases. Photography was an important part of document examination, and Kay needed an assistant to develop, print, and enlarge films. When Nard and Charlie finally decided it was time for Jane to go to work, Kay chose her for the job.

The publicity following Kay's success in identifying the typewritten extortion notes sent to the four society brides had brought her services as a handwriting expert into sudden demand.

While Nard rarely had the opportunity to appear in court, Kay often testified — on cases such as those involving the validity of a will, a signature on an important document, or the identity of handwriting on a note threatening to blow up a building. To the news media, she had become a very hot item.

While ostensibly the crime lab was founded to clear up

Chicago's gang wars, gang killings were investigated mostly by
the ballistics or weapons identification department. Nard examined some gangster suspects on his polygraph, but most of the
cases I've come across are marked "inconclusive" or "dangerous."
However, Nard used to tell about one gangster who was so scared
and frustrated when confronted with his "guilty" polygram that
he suddenly went berserk, ripped the paper out of the machine,
tore it up, and swallowed the pieces. Many gang leaders were
rounded up, arrested, and tried for income tax evasion around
that time, as airtight evidence of their crimes of violence was not
forthcoming. Several, including Al Capone, were sent to "The
Rock," the penitentiary on Alcatraz Island in San Francisco Bay.
Also with the repeal of Prohibition in 1933, transporting and
selling liquor became legal. And while gangsters continued to
operate in other illegal fields, there was not the same urgency to
get them behind bars.

But plenty of other types of cases were brought to the crime
lab, and its scientific methods of investigation received international publicity.

I was still in New York, still married to Bob Echols and living
in the home of Bob's great-uncle, a delightful little old gentleman,
but forgetful. On several occasions Kay, Nard, or both visited us
there. After the Lindbergh baby was kidnaped, Nard came with
Colonel Goddard to "stand by in the event they were needed."
Although Nard wasn't called into the "most famous case of the
century," a couple of years later he received a visit from Mrs.
Bruno Richard Hauptmann, wife of the convicted kidnaper-
slayer of the baby. In Chicago to raise funds for her husband's
appeal, she visited the crime lab and asked to be tested on the lie
detector to see how it worked. She insisted that no questions be
asked pertaining to her husband's case. Nard complied, asking
only inconsequential questions and catching her in a lie about her
age. She agreed that the machine worked, but didn't request
further tests, either for herself or for her husband, who was later
executed.

Another time when Nard came to New York to tell bankers
about his methods of screening employees and job applicants, he
and Kay both stayed with us. One night a group of us had dinner
in Greenwich Village, then visited a gypsy winter quarters in
several connecting vacant storefronts. After we had bantered

awhile with the gypsies, a flirtatious gypsy girl persuaded Nard to have his fortune told.

With their reputation of stealing from non-gypsies and of being habitual liars, Nard had often wondered how gypsies would react on the lie detector. He didn't have his instrument with him, but he did have two twenty-dollar gold pieces in his pocket. (This was just before President Hoover called in all the gold.) To see how the girl would react, he showed them to her. Fascinated, she offered to charm the gold pieces to bring him good luck. Before telling his fortune, she said, Nard must tie the gold pieces in a handkerchief. She demonstrated—"Like so and like so." He followed her directions. Taking the handkerchief, she went through several sleight-of-hand maneuvers, extracted the gold pieces, and made the handkerchief look as though they were still inside. But Nard's eye was quicker than her hand. He grabbed her wrist and flashed his police badge. Instead of being scared, the girl laughed gaily. "It was just a joke," she assured him, handing back his gold pieces.

Her mood was contagious. We all laughed.

A few years after this incident, Nard had a call from the States Attorney's office. Would he be willing to give a lie test to a gypsy in an encampment on Chicago's West Side? The girl had been accused of stealing a large sum of money from her mother-in-law, Queen Elizabeth, ruler of the tribe.

At the gypsy encampment the women wore bright-colored gypsy costumes and told fortunes. The men, whose forebears had been horse traders, were in a similar business—trading automobiles.

Queen Elizabeth (called "Queen Lizzie") and her husband, King Gus, gave Nard the facts in the case. The queen had wrapped $8,900 (eight $1,000 bills and nine $100 bills) in rags and had sewn them in her pillow. After stealing the bills, the thief had sewn up her pillow again. The rags the bills had been wrapped in had been found sewn up in Diane's (her daughter-in-law's) pillow. Lizzie had no doubt that Diane was the thief.

King Gus didn't think so. "It could be anyone," he insisted. But like his wife, he was curious to see how the lie detector worked. He turned to Nard. "You find out."

So, with Diane's permission, Nard attached her to the lie detector as other gypsies and a man from the States Attorney's office crowded around. After his usual preamble and several nonsensitive questions, Nard asked if she knew who had taken the money from Queen Lizzie's pillow, had she taken it, had she ever stolen money from anyone, and finally, did she believe she could really tell fortunes.

Diane's record was bad. She lied on almost all the questions. When Nard pointed this out on the graph, she laughed. To her, like the girl in Greenwich Village, it was all a big joke. But after Nard urged her to take the tests seriously and reminded her she could be in real trouble, Diane confessed she'd stolen $35 from a lady after telling her fortune. At one time she'd stolen $300 from Queen Lizzie. Could she really tell fortunes? Sometimes yes, sometimes no. But she swore and crossed her heart that she hadn't touched the money sewn up in Lizzie's pillow.

During several more tests, the lie detector backed her up. Queen Lizzie became agitated; she'd been so positive Diane was guilty. But having watched the pens on the lie detector, now she was convinced she'd been wrong. But what to do? After a short conference with the king, she waved her hand imperiously and "ordered" Nard to examine all twenty-nine members of the tribe.

Another daughter-in-law was tested next, but she, too, ran an innocent record, at least regarding the bills in the pillow. And so it went with all the members of the tribe, including the king and queen. There were liars among them, all right, but none reacted specifically to the question, "Did you take the money from Lizzie's pillow?"

Even though he never learned who had stolen the money from Lizzie's pillow (someone suggested it might have been a non-gypsy), Nard considered the case a success. From all the tests run, he was convinced that even chronic liars react to specific questions on the lie detector. Besides, he and everyone involved had thoroughly enjoyed themselves.

CHAPTER 12

Kay's Fabulous Hillbilly Case

Nineteen thirty-three was the year of the Chicago World's Fair; some may still remember. The crime lab had an exhibit, and Nard was in charge of it. When Bob and I passed through on a trip to California and stopped off to see the World's Fair, Kay and Nard invited us to visit them and stay in their attractive new apartment.

Touring the fair, we were impressed immediately by the strange and picturesque illumination. The buildings were weird, asymmetrical, modernistic. I felt as though I had landed in some strange city on Mars. Equally bizarre, though more fascinating, were stories Nard and Kay told us about cases they'd recently worked on. A few weeks earlier, for instance, Kay had had a case that took her into a wild district in the Kentucky hills. A big mail-order house in Chicago had been receiving a rash of bad checks for merchandise sent to post offices of various hamlets in the hill country of Kentucky. After an investigation, the mail-order people concluded that the postmasters of these isolated hamlets were themselves sending in orders accompanied by forged checks, and that they had forged the names of people living in their districts. To check their findings, they took three hundred of the bad checks and the signatures of nine of the suspected postmasters to the crime lab to be analyzed.

They were turned over to Kay. It was her first big case. After examining and comparing the two sets of signatures under the microscope, Kay reported that the postmasters were innocent and that the checks had been forged by at least forty different people.

The mail-order people couldn't believe that so many of their customers were writing bad checks. After trying to have the U. S. postal inspectors look into the matter, they sent several private detectives to the Kentucky hills.

Hard-boiled, accustomed to dealing with Chicago gangsters and thugs, the detectives barged confidently into this isolated territory of hidden stills and bloody feuds. But after several days of blunt questions, they found themselves surrounded by poorly clad, unshaven, suspicious-eyed characters with rifles — who escorted them to the nearest railroad station. Back in Chicago, they reported to their bosses that there wasn't a chance of getting anything out of those hillbillies.

Kay, meanwhile, had not given up. She urged the mail-order people to send her down to those Kentucky hills and assured them *she'd* bring back the evidence. After warning her of the dangers and attempting to dissuade her, they finally agreed that she and her assistant, Jane, could go if they and Colonel Goddard signed releases freeing the company from all responsibility.

Jane and Kay left for the Kentucky hills on May 29, 1933. Kay had figured out how to approach the hill people to get their signatures. Learning that the hill people were extremely proud of their pure lineage, she decided that she and Jane would pose as university students making a genealogical survey. The people, naturally, would resent being questioned on their moonshine, feuds, forged checks — but on their ancestry?

And how right Kay proved to be!

There were few roads in the area. "Folks" lived mostly up creeks — Hell-for-Sartin, Bloody, Fighting, Widows Creek — the latter so named because widows lived along it; their men had been killed off "feudin'." Dressed in jeans and jackets that concealed their pistols, the two young women rented horses and started out on their great adventure.

The first person they met was a tobacco-chewing mountaineer blocking their path with a rifle. "Whoa there, sisters! Where do you reckon you-all are a-goin'?"

They told him about their survey. "We're gathering material for a thesis on the racial stock in this district," Jane piped up, her knees quivering. She'd been well coached. Kay added, "We've been told that in this section we'd find direct descendants of the early Americans — probably the only people in America un-tainted by foreign blood."

This brought a glow to the face of the bearded man. He reckoned as how he could help them. And when it started to rain, he invited them to his cabin to meet his wife and "young uns." During supper — corn bread and string beans — the two young women showed a particular interest in the children, writing their height, weight, and the color of their eyes and hair. After finishing their "survey," they asked their host to sign it. When he hesitated, Kay hastened to explain, "Otherwise our professors will think we've just made all this up."

And so Kay and Jane, meandering on horseback from one tumbledown shack to another, sharing meager meals with the inhabitants, sometimes sleeping in the lofts or on porches of the cabins, managed to get the signatures of scores of people who had sent forged checks to the Chicago mail-order house.

In one cabin they spotted a brand-new "talking machine"; in another, a modern kitchen range (it couldn't be used, because there was no gas); in another, an electric train with switches, signals, stations — but there was no electricity. They talked to a woman wearing a fancy evening gown — to cook in. Another bragged of her new sewing machine. And so it went. As they jotted down information on racial lineage and obtained those hard-won signatures, they also noted the whereabouts of mer-chandise, a hidden printing press used to print bogus money orders, and other discoveries they thought might interest the mail-order people. The young women felt they were trusted — and safe.

Their first hint of trouble came at a hamlet where a ten-year-old boy riding a mule leveled a rifle at them. "You-uns better get goin' quick," he warned. "You ain't foolin' us."

Had the people begun to suspect? Alert for any sign of danger, the women continued their work. But on the following day, they knew they were in danger. A dozen scowling hillbillies carrying rifles gathered around them. One grumbled, "Maybe you're what you say you are, and maybe you ain't." Another warned, "Some hotheads round here are gettin' mighty suspi-cious. They're just as liable as not to shoot you if you stay hereabouts."

Kay and Jane, in no mood to argue, decided the time had come to clear out. They returned their horses to the rental stable, and with several hundred genealogical reports tucked in their belts, hired two boys to drive them back to Chicago.

Two weeks later, at the crime lab, after studying the signatures and comparing them with signatures on the forged checks, Kay presented the executives of the mail-order house with conclusive evidence that fifty people, whose signatures she had, were responsible for most of the bad checks.

It was quite a story. But for years I wondered, "Did those hillbillies really know they'd committed crimes?" Jane Wilson, now a widow living in Wisconsin, told me recently that she and Kay felt the one who started the whole thing probably was a criminal who had told the others they could get anything they wanted out of the mail-order catalogue — clothes, radios, washing machines, toys — simply by writing "notes," as they called the forged checks. They were too ignorant to understand that what they were doing was criminal.

The Prisoner Who Raised Canaries

My favorite among Nard's cases is about a prisoner who raised canaries.

It began in 1928, when Marie Hayden, the attractive, intelligent proprietor of the Green Gypsy Aviary, in Minneapolis, answered an ad in a trade paper for a certain type of canary. Mrs. Hayden specialized in unusual breeds of canaries and owned many cup and trophy winners.

She received a reply from the bird's owner, a young man named Joseph Blazenzits. The unusual thing was his return address: Marquette Penitentiary, Michigan.

Mrs. Hayden showed the letter to a Mrs. Corwine, her good friend and fellow canary fancier, and from that moment, these two women found a new interest far more absorbing than breeding Green Gypsy Rollers and German and American Blue Ribbon Winners.

They started to correspond with their fellow canary fancier. At first, their letters were about the canary they bought from him. Then, they learned that he was serving a life sentence for murder and had been raising canaries in prison (one of the few hobbies permitted), and began asking Joe about his life. After quite a long correspondence, in which Joe revealed an educated mind and a fine character, the women became convinced that he was serving time for a crime he had not committed. They became so interested in his case that they made a trip to Michigan to visit him; then, convinced of his innocence, they started an amazing campaign to bring about his release.

Enlisting the aid of ministers, judges, professors of criminal

law, doctors, businessmen, and prison wardens, the two ladies
traveled to Detroit to talk with Joe's family, and to Washington to
consult with authorities. Finally, they read in a magazine about
the lie detector and wrote to Nard for particulars. They even went
to Nard's office to observe a case being run, and collected all the
material they could find on the subject. Convinced of the machine's accuracy, they finally prevailed on the authorities to have
Joe examined on the polygraph.

But before decribing the test, here is Joe's story:

He was born in Darda, Austria, February 7, 1900. When he
was twelve years old he came with his parents to America, where
they settled in Detroit. Soon Joe fell in with questionable company, and the police began keeping an eye on him and his pals.

In 1917 the police arrested Joe for larceny. He and some "bad
boys" were riding in a stolen automobile concealing some brass
stolen from a boxcar. Joe was sentenced to serve one to five years
in Michigan State Prison at Jackson. Later he was paroled.

His next brush with the police occurred in October 1918,
when two bandits held up the Redford Savings Bank in Redford,
then a suburb of Detroit. The banker, Thomas Houghten, had just
kicked shut the door of the vault when he crumpled under a
fusillade of bullets. A witness saw two youthful thugs dart from
the bank and gave their descriptions to the police. A few days
later Blazenzits was arrested and was convicted of murder, almost wholly on the strength of eyewitness identification. He was
sentenced to life imprisonment at age eighteen.

The following June, after his family had spent all its money
to win him a new trial, the trial was granted. But again Joe was
convicted and a life sentence imposed.

Four years later, with inside aid, Joe escaped from Michigan
State Prison and returned to Detroit, where he rejoined his gang.
Ten days later, police arrested him while he and armed compan-
ions were said to be awaiting the arrival of a chain grocer at his
place of business. Then Joe was transferred to Marquette Branch
Prison.

When Joe entered Marquette, he had the equivalent of a
sixth grade education. But Marquette, apparently, was an advanced prison. The warden took a special interest in Joe, encouraging him to study and take up a hobby. Joe also made

friends with the chaplain, who influenced his prison career. He became a model prisoner, subscribing to correspondence courses and studying English, history, drafting, and mathematics. He went as far as calculus in his studies and became so proficient that he corrected an error in a college textbook problem, which the author and the publisher later acknowledged and corrected. In addition to his studies, he'd taken an unusual interest in the hobby of raising canaries. In his letters he showed a great tenderness toward the little feathered prisoners in his cages.

When he started corresponding with Marie Hayden and Mrs. Corwine, Joe had been in prison ten years. Marie Hayden then took the lead in getting him released. She encouraged his studies and induced him to write articles on prison life and juvenile delinquency. She contacted newspapers and magazines and had these articles published. Meanwhile, as a result of his studies, Joe became an able draftsman and architect and designed the first model prison rehabilitation camp for first offenders, which the state later built at Hartford.

For five years Marie Hayden tirelessly collected evidence that might gain Joe's release. She presented his file to noted criminal lawyers and peace officers in several states, who generally concurred that the evidence left strong doubt of Joe's guilt. But the wheels of justice ground slowly.

It was 1933 when Marie Hayden prevailed on the state parole commissioner to have Joe tested on the lie detector. The commissioner consented, and taking his portable machine to Marquette Penitentiary, Nard tested Joe in front of the parole commissioner, the warden, and other law enforcement agents. An alibi witness for Joe, who claimed to have been with him several miles from the scene at the time of the Redford Bank robbery and murder, was also tested.

Here are the questions Joe was asked:

1. Is your name Blazenzits?

   A. Yes.

2. You are an inmate here in the penitentiary?

   A. Yes

3. Do you know who killed Houghten?

   A. No.

4. Did you kill Houghten?

   A. No.

5. Did you have lunch today?

   A. Yes.

6. Were you ever on a stick-up with a friend?

   A. Yes.

7. Were you with that friend the night Houghten was killed?

   A. Yes.

8. Did you participate in the stick-up on the night of Houghten's death?

   (His answer was unintelligible.)

9. Did you shoot Houghten?

   A. No.

10. You get along with the prisoners here?

    A. Yes.

11. Do you like the food here?

    A. Some of it.

After these tests and the test on the alibi witness, Nard stated: "I feel sure Blazenzits had no part in this murder for which he is now serving time."

The newspapers reported that Joe's reaction to the question "Do you like the food here?" was stronger than his reaction to the Houghten slaying.

Afterward, Nard wrote to Marie Hayden, with whom he had

had considerable correspondence on the case and had come to know as a friend. Here, in part, is what he said:

> In conducting the test on Joe, I felt that it would be far better to let the commissioner know that we were interested in finding the whole truth as to Joe's past, i.e., the part pertaining to his criminal career, so that he, the commissioner, would not think that we were trying to cover up or only bring out Joe's good qualities. If we had asked questions pertaining only to the Houghten murder and not gone into the escape or his association with his alibi witness friend, it would have looked to the commissioner as though we were trying to "whitewash" Joe and make him a pure, white angel which, of course, would have caused the commissioner to respond unfavorably to the test. After all, when a man is brought before the parole commissioner for consideration of parole or pardon, the commissioner delves into the individual's previous behavior regardless of the crime for which he is serving time, and I felt that it would be much better to bring out that history in an impartial way before the commissioner at the time of the test.
>
> Furthermore, I was desirous of obtaining some significant response to some question in order to show that Joe was responsive and that some lesser crime or point of embarrassment would produce a greater reaction on the machine than would have been obtained to questions pertaining to the murder of Houghten. This, I felt sure, would be quite convincing and would make the test self-explanatory to the commissioner.

Through Marie Hayden's efforts, a tremendous amount of pressure from all over the country had been brought to bear on the Blazenzits case. Some of the nation's top lawyers had read records of Joe's case and transcripts of the trial and had wired the Michigan Prison commissioner for clemency. So after the lie test, which received wide publicity, it was evident that something had to be done — that Joe would be either paroled or pardoned.

But the U. S. immigration authorities claimed that on parole, Joe would be deportable to his native Austria because he had once made an excursion to Bob-Lo, a Canadian-owned island in the Detroit River. With a pardon, however, Joe would be free to start a new life as an American citizen.

Curiously, Joe's mother, who had spent all her money trying to release her son when he was first convicted, became worried when, after fifteen years in prison, it appeared he might be pardoned. She was afraid that he really had committed the murder and that he might take another life — a crime for which she, as his mother, would feel responsible. Marie Hayden persuaded Nard to talk to Joe's mother and convince her that Joe was really innocent.

After the test, the parole commissioner said he was not convinced of the lie detector's infallibility. But in his report to the governor, recommending a pardon for Joe, he quoted Nard's words as justification for releasing Joe. The foreman of the jury that had convicted Joe the second time expressed doubt that Joe was guilty and said he had voted for acquittal three times but had at last given in to the other jurors. The judge who had sentenced Joe to life imprisonment stated that "no doubt the company Joe kept convinced the jury he was a bad boy."

The final testimony that helped to release Joe came from the physician who had attended Houghten before he died. He wrote an affidavit saying that on his deathbed Houghten had told him he was shot by a robber who had entered his bank to commit a robbery a year previously.

And so, after five years of continuous effort and voluminous correspondence, Marie Hayden at last secured a full pardon from Governor Comstock for her protege, Joe Blazenzits.

Joe had become so valuable to the prison in his work of designing the rehabilitation camp for first offenders, however, that the warden asked if he would keep working on the project as a private citizen. Joe consented and finished the job. Afterward he went to Minneapolis and asked the lady who had secured his release to become his wife.

Since that time, Joe and Marie Blazenzits have worked as a team, writing articles and stories on crime, criminals, prisons, and how to save boys from stumbling along the wrong road. As for the little canary who brought them together, the records don't say what happened to him.

CHAPTER 14

Coal Mine Bombing

Nard and Kay and Charlie and Jane were very close. They worked together, played together, and sometimes fought together. At least Nard and Charlie fought. Their disputes and arguments were not so much a matter of rivalry as of honest differences of opinion. In today's terms, Nard was a dove, Charlie a hawk. As Jane used to say, when a nice guy was needed, Nard took the case; when a tough guy was called for, it was usually Charlie. Their bickering served as a balancing force, prodding Nard into more aggressiveness; damping down the belligerence in Charlie. They made a great team, working together on hundreds of cases.

In 1934, in the depth of the Depression, Burt Massee, the founder of the crime lab and its chief backer, underwent financial reverses. Funds for the laboratory dropped off sharply. There was not enough money to pay the generous salary of Colonel Goddard, who took a leave of absence and resigned a year later.

In the interim the lab was headed, successively, by two professors at Northwestern, then by Nard, who became the director for about three years. Charlie, his right-hand man, devoted an increasing amount of time to Colonel Goddard's specialty — the identification of firearms, ammunition, and explosives. Nard continued to run cases on the lie detector, by now with two assistants and two additional polygraphs. The experts in other fields worked more or less independently, collaborating when the cases called for it.

Despite the cutbacks, business for this nonprofit organization was booming. Every type of case one could dream up was

brought in, including one involving the purported mummy of
John Wilkes Booth. The mummy was being shown at fairs and
carnivals, and, after lie tests, the owners "conceded" it was a
fraud.

By 1935, gang wars had eased off, but with millions of
workers jobless and many thousands of jobholders earning star-
vation wages, labor wars began to erupt. In connection with
hostilities between two rival mine workers' unions, Nard, Charlie, and the entire crime lab staff combined their talents. For a
long period, murders, assaults, and bombings had terrorized
people in the mining area of southern Illinois.

One August night at 2:05 a.m., this war reached a climax. A
huge bomb exploded, blowing up the power house at one of the
mines.

Early the next morning the telephone woke Nard. It was T. P.
Sullivan, head of the Bureau of Identification and Investigation
for the state of Illinois. After describing the explosion, he said the
state police wanted to make this case an example. They wanted
every means of scientific investigation used to track down the
perpetrators, bring them to justice, and prevent similar acts of
violence in the future.

Nard asked Kay to alert all the members of the crime lab
staff. Then he picked up Charlie, and the two men headed for
southern Illinois.

Meanwhile, the president of the bombed mine ordered his
men to rope off the entire explosion site and post a guard. Thanks
to his foresight, all the evidence was saved, enabling the experts
at the crime lab to build the first all-scientific case in the history
of American prosecution.

When Nard and Charlie arrived, the fumes from the explosion had barely dissipated. The power house was a pile of rubble;
the scene, utter devastation. After conferring with the authorities, Nard and Charlie moved slowly about in the roped-off
area, picking up bits of tin, a piece of charred string, adhesive
tape, pieces of wire, an alarm clock rigged up as a time-bomb
mechanism, and other scraps of evidence.

As they sorted through the rubble, the FBI and state and
private investigators began to congregate. Soon they began to
round up suspects, raid hideouts, and jail professional agitators
and known troublemakers.

With the scraps and pieces they'd salvaged, Nard and Charlie rushed back to the crime lab, where the experts set to work immediately, photographing, enlarging, and making chemical analyses and ultra-violet ray examinations of the evidence.

Within the next few days, dozens of suspects were brought to the crime lab for lie detector tests. Through the polygrams, conversations, and confessions that followed, Nard and his assistants learned that during the two-year labor war, there had been some twenty-six murders, scores of clubbings and beatings, and numerous bombings.

But in spite of these dramatic revelations, Nard, following T. P. Sullivan's directive, concentrated on the coal mine explosion itself. After days of questioning, he finally narrowed the suspects down to four — Mitch, Bob, Joe, and Pete. The first three ran decidedly suspicious records, and Nard felt sure the fourth, Pete, was connected with the case, although he couldn't get a clear-cut deceptive polygram. When Nard explained his frustration over his odd and indecisive graphs, Pete broke down and told all. A nice-looking young man of twenty-six, he lived in a rented room in the mining town of Valier not far from the mine and powerhouse that had been bombed. But he was not a miner. A few years before, he'd been arrested for making counterfeit quarters; after three years in prison, he had only just been paroled. Likeable and smart, Pete had the reputation among his friends of being a genius at building and repairing radios. They could not understand how he could have done such a foolish thing as make counterfeit money.

One day Pete was watching workmen put up telephone lines, and struck up a conversation with Mitch, a miner who lived nearby. The two men soon discovered they were both interested in the same hobby — radio and electricity.

From then on, they met frequently to discuss their common interests. Mitch introduced Pete to two of his miner friends, Bob and Joe, and soon the four men started meeting at Joe's house to play cards. The three miners often discussed their activities at work. Mitch and Bob were chairmen of strike committees. Bob didn't always attend the card games, and Pete didn't know him as well as the others.

Since being paroled, Pete hadn't found a job. His friends tried to help him, but few jobs were available. At one of the games, Pete asked Mitch if he wouldn't like to go into the radio repair business with him. Mitch and the other men thought it was a great idea. Joe, the host, offered to have the business right there in his house; Pete could rent a room there for $1.00 a month and pay the electric bill, which came to only about $1.50.

So it was arranged. Pete's mother gave him some money for equipment. Mitch put up $12.00 for radio tubes.

Pete did well with his business and managed to stay out of trouble. He reported regularly to his parole board and avoided bars and ex-cons. His absorbing interest seemed to be radio.

One afternoon Bob stopped by Pete's shop to pick up an automobile radio that he'd left to be repaired. The men talked awhile about the radio, then Bob said he had to go. Pete went with him to the front porch. Then, offhandedly as though he'd just thought of it, Bob asked Pete if he could fix a clock so it would complete an electric circuit when set at a certain time.

Pete nodded. He'd made one before to turn a radio on and off.

"How did you do it?" Bob asked.

"When an alarm goes off, the alarm key revolves in the opposite direction to which it's wound," Pete explained. "Take an alarm clock and fasten it to a wooden base, and fasten a metal rod to the alarm key." He continued on through a long, complicated explanation which Bob seemed to understand. When Pete had finished, Bob thanked him and left, explaining he might need something like that someday.

Several months later Pete was at Mitch's house when Bob happened by. Pete and Bob started talking again about electrical devices, and Bob asked, casually, how he could fix up a switch to be placed on a rail so as to complete an electric circuit when the wheel of a railroad car passed over it. Pete told him he didn't know of any such switch, but suggested using a push button, the kind used for doorbells.

Bob didn't seem to go for this. Eager to help, Pete persisted: "What's it for?"

"Oh, skip it," Bob said and left abruptly.

But later in the week he dropped by Pete's radio shop saying he wanted to talk privately. Pete suggested they go outside. In a low voice, Bob told Pete they still wanted him to think up something to use as a switch. The only solution, Pete said finally, was to take a twisted wire and wrap it around that rail, so that when the wheel of the car passed over it, it would crush the insulation and press the two leads together, completing the circuit.

He took Bob to the garage behind the house to show him how it worked.

Aware by now that Bob wouldn't want to discuss what he planned to use this for, Pete didn't ask questions. But he soon found out. When police searched his room, they found newspaper clippings about bombings, train wrecks, and other "accidents" circled in red ink.

Pete admitted other incidents to Nard and retold them at the trial.

One day, when feelings were running high between the two rival unions, Mitch told Pete he'd been terribly worried about his car. The night before he'd run it into a ditch and had finally gotten Joe to help push it out. It would have been too bad if anyone had found what was in the car, he said. While the car was ditched, he had to remove all the stuff and put it in the bushes.

Pete had been around his miner friends long enough to know "stuff" meant dynamite.

Another time, he heard Bob say that So-and-so was a good man, but too jittery when he went out on a job — always afraid someone might be hurt or killed.

But despite the questions he was asked and the information dropped in his presence, Pete still behaved himself and reported regularly to his parole board.

For several weeks, everything at the mines was calm. Then two bills came before the state legislature to give miners shorter hours and a pay raise. The miners thought they'd be passed, but when they weren't, Pete overheard Mitch tell Bob that the only thing left was to increase the cost of production in the mines by destroying property. This would force the coal companies to replace the men who were out of work.

On still another occasion, Mitch invited Pete to a picnic for unemployed miners, held in the woods near the site of the subsequent explosion. During the day, Mitch walked around the power house and drove under a nearby bridge. On his return, he told Pete that he was surprised to find no guard on duty. "Wow!" he exclaimed. "Would that be easy to blow up!"

At the trial, Pete testified that when he learned of the

tremendous mine explosion, he'd been pretty sure that it had something to do with Mitch's statements. But, the newspapers reported that Pete's testimony at that famous trial "did not have the dramatic force of the story revealed by science — the hidden truth laid bare by chemistry, photography, microscopy, and the lie detector." This was the big story, followed intently by criminologists and law enforcement agencies all over the country.

For not only were four suspects on trial, but science itself was on trial.

The experts at the crime lab became key witnesses for the state. Nard decribed the results of his lie detector tests. Charlie proved that wire on what was left of the bomb mechanism had been taken from a length of wire found in the home of one of the defendants; photographed through a comparison microscope, magnified fifty-five diameters, and lined up, the wires showed innumerable points of similarity. The adhesive tape found on the bomb came from a roll of adhesive in the home of one of the defendants, as Kay proved with photographs enlarged 529 times. Another expert identified a piece of cord. And Dr. Edwin O'Neill, a staff member, proved scientifically that a certain type of time bomb had blown up the power house.

Through the mass of scientific evidence and Nard's lie detector reports, which had singled out the four suspects, the two-year reign of terror in the southern Illinois coal mines came to an end. Mitch and Bob were convicted and sent to prison. Joe, host at the card games, apparently knew what was going on but did not take part in the actual crimes. As for Pete, apparently it was not illegal for a man to own a radio repair shop and share his technical knowledge with his most favored customers, regardless of how that knowledge may have been put to use.

The Wichita Cases

By the spring of 1935, Nard was so busy running cases on the polygraph and traveling about the country investigating robberies and murders that he could hardly tell one week from another.

But in the event of a family emergency, he somehow managed to be there. Either Charlie Wilson or Fred Inbau, another associate who had studied with him, could take charge at the lab.

Nard must have gleaned from my letters that I was having trouble. He just "happened" to be in New York at the time Bob and I broke up. After talks with us both, Nard urged me to come west. "Kay and I are driving to California. We'll take you along."

There were four of us on that cross-country trek — Nard, Kay, me, and Chief — not Chief Vollmer, but his namesake, a four-month-old German shepherd pup. On the trip west, Kay spent most of her time training Chief at the rate of two or three new commands each day. When he'd grab her hat or tug at her handbag, quietly, without raising her voice, Kay would get him to repeat these acts on command, then reward him with praise. Over the next few years, under Kay's tutelage, Chief became a "wonder dog," like Stronghart and Rin-tin-tin. He understood and obeyed some one hundred commands. Nard made boxing gloves for him and boxed with him. Twice, after Nard and Kay decided it was easier to use taxis in Chicago than own a car, Chief climbed into a taxi on his own when he'd escaped from his dog-walker. Getting Chief's address from his metal name tag, the cabbies brought him home and collected the fare.

Chief—Nard and Kay's German Shepherd.

To get back to our cross-country jaunt, relatives and family friends had urged Nard to come to California. Father had just had part of his thyroid gland removed and Ormeida wasn't well. They were having financial problems.

But despite the urgency, Nard insisted we should take in all the sights along the way. He needed a vacation from crime, criminals, responsibilities. After exploring Tom Sawyer's cave at Hannibal, Missouri, we headed for Wichita, Kansas, where O. W. Wilson, the chief of police, had invited Nard to stay. Chief Wilson had formerly worked under Chief Vollmer in Berkeley, and the two were close friends. O. W., as Nard called him, championed the lie detector and Nard's work. Since they had much to discuss, Kay and I stayed with other friends.

This visit started out calmly enough. We attended a demonstration of trained Doberman pinschers. Obedience training was in its infancy then. A few police departments, including the Berkeley police, were experimenting with dog patrol units, and Nard and Kay were interested in this new development. (For many years dogs had been used for police work in Germany and other European countries.)

On the third day of our visit, which we thought would be the last, the captain of detectives, knowing Nard and Kay were in town, asked O. W. if they might be willing to help out on a case. It turned out to be quite sensational.

A few days before we reached Wichita, Fred Dold, Jr., the superintendent of a large food-processing plant, who was also the owner's son, received a scrawled, illiterate note in the morning mail:

> I want $2,500 by 6 p.m. Tuesday, May 28, 1935 or your plant will be blown to bits. I have place 2 gallons nitroglycerine in your plant. Do not go to the police for I work for you now and your every move will be watched. See this is no idle threat. I mean business. I am the only one that can remove the nitroglycerine so do not look for it. I will remove it when I receive the money.

Directions followed on how to reach a certain spot on the outskirts of the city.

> Leave money by elm tree. The time is set for the nitro to go off. I want 200 $10 bills 100 $5 bills 500 $1 bills. Leave money at 6 p.m. sharp and I will stop the nitro from going off . . . if you leave a dummy package I will know and your plant will be blown to hell. All the police cannot stop it . . . I am the only one so if I am caught your plant will go just the same. Leave money and save your plant . . . rap money in newspaper. *Do not go to the police if you want your plant . . . see.*

As Dold put down the note, his hand was shaking. His father, eighty-six, now retired, had a heart condition; a shock like this could kill him. The plant, covering several acres, employed some six hundred workers. If two gallons of nitroglycerine were indeed hidden on the premises, all of them were in jeopardy.

Ignoring the extortionist's warning, the superintendent telephoned police headquarters, almost incoherent. He wailed, "They're going to kill me! Blow up the plant! Kill us all!"

Thomas Jaycox, the detective who answered the phone replied calmly. "Just hold everything. I'll be right over."

After reading the extortion note, held carefully by one corner to preserve fingerprints, Jaycox concluded that the extortionist must be a crank or a disgruntled employee. But, whoever he was, he meant business. It was nine a.m. now, with nine hours to go until the bomb was set to go off.

On a hunch, the detective added up the sums asked for in the note. "Uh, oh! Something wrong here. He wants $2,500 in bills. But the bills he asks for add up to $3,000!"

"Why didn't he ask for more money?" the superintendent asked.

"It's an amount he thinks he can get," the detective replied. Then Jaycox called police headquarters and asked to have ten of his top men sent to the plant immediately. Next, he instructed the superintendent to pick ten of his most reliable men. Quietly, so as not to cause panic, they were to search the entire plant, area by area, every possible hiding place until the bomb was found.

When the men were assembled, Dold joined the search himself. Fanning out, the men looked through shelves and cupboards, inspected machinery, conveyer belts, huge refrigerated areas, even the boiler room, where, in all that heat, the nitro surely would have already exploded.

As the search continued into every cranny, the detective slipped out. Wearing a white company coat and driving a company car, he followed the directions in the note for several miles until he spotted the elm tree. If the extortionist was watching, he reasoned, he'd think he was the superintendent looking over the place where the money was to be dropped.

Returning around noon, Jaycox learned that no bomb had yet been found and that there were still vast storage areas piled high with cartons, any one of which might contain the nitro. He asked the superintendent to tell all his foremen the truth (they all suspected something by now) and recruit their most reliable men to augment the search.

Detective Jaycox then returned to police headquarters, changed clothes, and picked up a partner and a plainclothes "chauffeur." In an unmarked car, dressed like hitchhikers with backpacks, carrying army blankets wrapped around sawed-off shotguns, the two officers were driven to within two miles of the elm tree.

For half an hour, the two police officers tramped up the road, scanning the countryside for unusual activity. Finally they came to a settlement of small houses and businesses. Across the road, on a hill, was the elm tree. They walked several hundred yards beyond it, then ducked into a cornfield and crept along the ground until they were a few yards from the elm. There they lay, hour after hour, fighting off flies and mosquitoes, waiting.

The road they had come on was muddy, and the stretch nearest the elm impassable. During the whole afternoon no cars or people passed by. Then, just as the six o'clock whistles blew, a car drove up the road to the muddy section, It was Fred Dold, Jr., the superintendent, come to deliver the money. He sloshed up the road, crossed to the hill, climbed it, and dropped a package tied with red string under the elm tree, strode back to his car, and sped off.

Again the police officers waited. Had the plant blown up, they would have heard it — two gallons of nitro were ten times more than enough to demolish the entire plant, and the blast would be heard for miles. But the deadline had passed. No bomb had exploded. The search would be over and all the workers would have gone home.

Minutes passed. The hearts of the two men beat faster.

At 6:20, a young man wearing overalls with a spade over his shoulder, holding the hand of a small boy, sauntered up the road. The man seemed to be looking for something. The officers tensed. Could this innocent-looking fellow possibly be the mad extortionist?

The man left the road and clumped up the hill toward the elm, the boy tagging along. A few feet from the package, he stopped and looked around. Then, as he bent down to pick it up, the police officers sprang to their feet.

"Who are you?" the man stuttered. "W-what do you want of me?"

"We're police officers," Jaycox said. "What are you doing up here?"

The man explained that he was looking for a small tree to plant in his yard. He'd gotten several here before. He lived just over there, he said, pointing to the settlement across the road.

He seemed harmless enough, but the timing was too pat. The officers couldn't take a chance. "We're taking you to police headquarters."

They dropped the little boy off at a grocery store in the settlement and told him to go home and tell his mother his dad had gone downtown.

On the way to the police station, the suspect, who said his name was William H. Smith, became excited. His wife was sick, he said, and he threatened to sue the officers. Afraid of making a mistake, the officers took Smith home to talk briefly to his wife and his sister, who lived with them.

At the police station they questioned Smith late into the night. But he stuck to his story. An officer dispatched to his home reported that recently several small trees had been planted in Smith's yard, and a hole was dug for another.

By now, Jaycox was almost convinced he had brought in the wrong man. Then he began questioning Smith about his job. He worked for the W. P. A. and explained that in his time off he was an inventor. Asked what he invented, Smith's face flushed and his eyes lit. He went into a long, rambling explanation of his perpetual-motion machine. "When I get it finished, it will take the place of gasoline for cars!"

This really convinced his interrogators that their suspect was just a harmless crackpot, but, unwittingly, Smith added, "I can't finish till I get $2,500" — the exact amount demanded in the extortion note!

Unaware of his blooper, Smith continued to answer questions until at last he was bedded down in a jail cell.

The next morning, his wife and sister came to the police station demanding his immediate release. Without further evidence, Smith could be held only one more day — until five o'clock that evening. Either he would be charged with the crime or released from custody.

Feeling certain now that Smith or a member of his family had written the extortion note, Jaycox obtained samples of writing and printing from him, his wife, and his sister. These samples were sent to J. Curtis Shearman, a handwriting expert in Wichita. Shearman reported that the original note and all the samples were so well disguised that he couldn't make an identification until he could get undisguised samples. This would take at least another day. So, at five o'clock, Smith was released.

The case had reached this point when Jaycox learned the Keelers were in Wichita and, through Chief Wilson, asked them to help. So the following morning, Nard, Kay, and Shearman, whom Nard already knew and liked, met at the police station. Smith had already been brought in.

First, Kay and Shearman worked together getting undisguised samples of Smith's handwriting and printing. Then, with Chief Wilson assisting, Nard gave Smith several lie detector tests.

Kay's and Shearman's findings were that Smith had written the extortion note himself; Nard's, that he had lied on all the tests. He not only wrote the note but mailed it and went to collect the money.

In an office next to the interrogation room, Nard spread out a strip of paper he'd taken from the polygraph, and pointed to various places on the graph as he explained it to the police officers who had worked on the case. "His blood pressure began to rise after the third question — 'Did you send the threatening letter?' And it continued to rise until it reached a peak — here. When I asked, finally, 'Have you told me the truth as you know it?' Smith answered 'Yes,' but the sudden rise here, followed by a sharp drop, was a decisive indication that he was *not* telling the truth."

Nard returned to the interrogation room, and all that afternoon he and Chief Wilson continued to question Smith, both on and off the detector. They explained the graphs to him, pointing out the peaks where he had lied, the drops indicating relief. Finally, at seven o'clock, worn out, Smith admitted he'd had enough. He confessed that he'd written the extortion letter, bought an envelope downtown, and mailed it at the post office. No one else had any part in it. He'd disguised his printing and used an envelope that he knew could not be traced. The little boy and the spade were coverups. He wasn't looking for a small tree, but for the payoff money. The nitroglycerine was a bluff. It didn't exist.

As Jaycox read the confession, he smiled grimly. He'd been right about Smith from the start. But what a waste — all those hours spent searching the plant — those frayed nerves! And Chief Wilson admitted that if it hadn't been for Kay's and Shearman's handwriting expertise, showing how a person's normal writing habits creep into even carefully disguised writing, and Nard's lie detector tests, Smith's guilt might have gone unproved.

To Nard and Kay, it was just another case. When Kay came home late that night, all she said was "We got a confession" and went to bed. Even the next morning, after we'd thanked our hosts and were back on the highway, Nard was so engrossed in telling Kay about a new experiment he planned that he barely referred to the extortion case.

On the last lap of our trip, Nard stopped here and there to see friends — an artist in Santa Fe, a writer in Taos, a retired actor then in the souvenir business. He knew people all over the country. We visited Indian ruins, swam in Great Salt Lake, caught a glimpse of the Grand Canyon. Every day Nard called the crime lab and father to see how things were going. And he didn't get involved in any more crimes or with any more criminologists until we reached Berkeley. Then, between visits with father, our stepmother, and old friends, he spent the rest of his time with Chief Vollmer and his police-officer friends at the Berkeley Police Department.

Father was delighted to see us, but he wouldn't even consider Nard's proposals — moving to smaller quarters to save work and money and having an expert handle his finances. He was working on a book, he told us, which he expected to sell. We were skeptical, although recently, more than forty years after father's death, several of his books are being published.

Kay had left us in Pocatello, Idaho, to drive with her sister-in-law to visit her family in Walla Walla, Washington. The second week of our visit, Nard went fishing with Uncle Sterling, while I took care of Chief. Then they were all back with Kay's teenage brother, Teddy, in tow, and after a few more days, with Nard's friends dropping in and the telephone ringing incessantly, we all hugged and kissed and shouted good-bye and Nard, Kay, Teddy, and Chief were off in a whirl to Chicago.

It hadn't been a very restful visit for father and our step-mother. But they appreciated Nard's coming, even though he attracted such crowds of people and brought a dog who, for all his cleverness, was not fully house-trained.

Although, in the following years, I saw Nard from time to time, that trip west was our last long visit — until after the plane crash. But I have his journals, letters, news clippings, and case histories to help me reconstruct those long periods when we were apart.

The following spring, Nard returned to Wichita to work on an experimental project Chief O. W. Wilson had outlined to him. Meanwhile, O. W. had bought one of Nard's lie detectors. His goal was to make Wichita as crime-free as Berkeley had been during Chief Vollmer's years. But, as O. W. explained to Nard, the problems in Wichita, a farming center, were vastly different from those of Berkeley. During the harvest season, hordes of itinerant workers poured through the city. Most were all right, but among them were drifters, some with criminal records, who posed a menace to the entire area.

Nard and O. W. discussed how to screen these men. They needed a pretext to pick up the men and get them to consent to a lie test. Finally they hit on a scheme. Men who arrived in town by hitchhiking or hopping a freight, or who were found under dubious circumstances, would be questioned by the police. If they seemed suspicious, they'd be arrested and taken to police head-quarters. Their belongings would be searched, and anyone who had a gun, knife, or other weapon would be held on that offense. Their fingerprints would be taken and sent to the FBI in Washington. Then these men would be told they could either stay in jail for a week to ten days while waiting for their fingerprint reports, or take a lie detector test. When the program got under way, Nard found that practically all the men would rather take a lie test than stay in jail.

So he got a great number of polygrams.

While some critics thought the experiment was an invasion of human rights, some of the vagrants actually benefited from it. Officers making the arrests would become interested in them, treat them to meals, even lend them money. And men kept overnight in jail were often grateful for the two free meals and a clean bed. Unless they were wanted for an offense, they were released the following day but told to get out of town.

Those who had committed some offense were kept in jail until their court trials. If wanted in some other town, they were held until the police there took them into custody or reported that they were no longer wanted.

As a result of the experiment, crime in Wichita was considerably reduced. The polygraph examiner at the police station worked with Nard and, after Nard left, carried on the tests.

One phase of the project delighted Nard. Many of the men told fascinating stories, often dramatic or pathetic, of their lives on the bum. When they'd let it all out, they seemed relieved, as though their consciences had been cleared. So eventually, what had been called the "vagrant's court" became known as an "ease your conscience service."

For example, Nard took a particular interest in the case of one runaway boy, only fourteen or fifteen years old, who'd left his home in a neighboring state to take a farm job and was picked up for hitchhiking. The boy's record on the lie detector was bad. After Nard explained the peaks and dips on the graph, he admitted a whole string of thefts. He'd stolen hay for his calf; he'd stolen a tire pump and some blackberries; once he'd done some shoplifting, taken a pair of socks and other things. All were minor offenses, but they weighed on his conscience. After the boy told all, Nard tested him again and he ran a clear record. When he saw the difference between his last and first records, a big grin spread over the boy's face and he said, "Gee! I guess I can go back home now!"

This was the type of case Nard really enjoyed, in which the polygraph helped potential criminals turn about, go straight, and lead productive lives. And in the course of his career, Nard and his magic black box helped a great many individuals, often in unexpected ways.

But there were some he couldn't help.

CHAPTER 16

Grim Electrocution

Nineteen thirty-six was a good year for Nard. His blood pressure was still fairly normal, his spirits high, and his reputation soaring. An article about him in *McCall's* magazine was reprinted in the *Reader's Digest;* he appeared in the movies on the *The March of Time;* he gave numerous lectures and radio talks. Already reporters were calling him world-famous.

He and Burt Massee had become close friends. Through Burt, Nard became acquainted with other prominent businessmen, including Commander Eugene McDonald, president of the Zenith Radio Corporation. He and Kay were invited to glamorous social functions, where, with his special charm and gift for storytelling, Nard was often the star. As for Kay, while she enjoyed matching wits with the successful and famous, she preferred more relaxed gatherings with Charlie, Jane and her friends. Nard's social life was creating a growing rift between them. I'd sensed on our trip west that something was wrong. But both were anxious to patch up their differences.

Soon after Nard's return from his project with the Wichita vagrants, Kay read an article by Commander McDonald on how a person could go yachting at very small expense. Nard and Kay had often gone boating with friends on Lake Michigan, and both loved the water. Now they decided to get a yacht of their own.

The "yacht" turned out to be a second-hand, twenty-two-foot speedboat without sleeping cabins or facilities, for which they paid $400.00. They named it the *Walla Walla,* after Kay's hometown. And from then on, every day after work, they'd pick up Chief and go down to the lakefront, to work on the boat, swim, aquaplane, or ride around exploring caves and inlets.

In August, Nard, Kay, Chief and two friends, Dr. and Mrs. Humiston of Northwestern University, started on a month's cruise of the Great Lakes. Every night on this 1,400-hundred-mile trip they had to tie up their boat at a dock, put up pup tents for each couple to sleep in (Chief slept outside to guard the boat) and cook over an open fire. With an automobile compass, they followed a dotted line on their map and stopped at many ports for gas, supplies, and sightseeing. Their destination was a camp in the Canadian wilds at McGregor Bay, where, according to Kay's journal, they fished, swam, climbed steep and rocky hillsides, explored hidden lakes in rented canoes, and "watched a city dog go into ecstasies of leaping, swimming, and sniffing in the woods."

On their way home, near Escanaba, Michigan, they saw a boat in the distance that they soon recognized as the *Mizpah;* Commander McDonald's yacht, referred to by reporters as "palatial." It had a crew of thirty. At the same moment, Commander McDonald, who knew Nard and Kay were in the area, saw a far-off speck in the water and soon realized it was their boat. The two boats approached, until together they drew into Escanaba. Burt Massee, his wife and son, and Commander McDonald's young wife and two children were all aboard. The McDonalds invited Nard and his party for dinner, and as they had a long journey ahead, the commander offered to have the *Walla Walla* hoisted up onto their yacht so Nard, Kay, and their guests could sail home in comfort. Nard and Kay declined that invitation, preferring to finish their adventure on their own.

During most of the cruise, they'd had clear weather and calm water, but toward the end there were high waves. Kay wrote: "Our boat leaped across the waves, and some people who saw us said we were actually out of the water some of the time." But they had life preservers — even Chief had a life preserver — and they managed to get home safely.

That trip must have been a very special time; perhaps the last really happy vacation Kay and Nard had together. From then on problems began to mount.

Usually Nard was selective about the cases he took on. But

once he was pressured into working on a sensational case that proved disastrous — at least, to his peace of mind.

On the morning of March 2, 1937, garish headlines like these appeared coast to coast:

LIE DETECTOR SENDS KILLER TO HIS DEATH
A NEEDLE'S JUMP CONDEMNS A MAN TO DEATH IN THE
ELECTRIC CHAIR
LIE TESTER IS KILLER'S NEMESIS
LIE DETECTOR FAILS TO SAVE YOUNG CONVICT

The stories under these headlines (of which only the last really told the truth) was essentially this:

A man condemned to death for murder had just seven hours to live before being executed in the electric chair at the Cook County Jail. Arriving in Chicago, Governor Henry Horner of Illinois was accosted in the crowded railway station by the condemned man's younger sister, who sobbed and pleaded with him to save her brother's life. Torn between compassion and duty, the governor explained that he had already granted six stays of execution and that it was against his conscience to grant another. But as the girl pursued her frantic appeal, he relented somewhat, murmuring something about having great faith in the lie detector.

Clutching at this straw, the sister dashed to the office of her brother's lawyer. The lawyer, who had exhausted every judicial recourse, agreed to accompany her to Governor Horner's hotel suite, where again the girl pleaded — this time for the governor to arrange a lie detector test for her brother. After conferring with both his own lawyer and the lawyer for the condemned man, the governor finally gave the go-ahead.

Governor Horner was a good friend, whom Nard respected. While it was against his better judgment, he agreed to run the test. But there was another hindrance. The warden of the Cook County Jail insisted on a court order. So the sister and her brother's lawyer raced miles away to get a municipal judge to sign the necessary order permitting the test.

By the time Nard arrived at the jail carrying his black box, the prisoner had only four hours left to live. Nard had to give the test under the very worst circumstances — in the prisoner's cell. The whole atmosphere was like a circus, he later said; reporters, lawyers, and prison and law enforcement officials crowded around. The condemned man's lawyer explained to him that this was his last chance. If this test showed that he was telling the truth when he affirmed he had not committed the murder, the governor might believe him innocent.

The prisoner agreed to take the test. After connecting him to the apparatus and giving his usual preamble, Nard took ten playing cards out of his pocket, shuffled them, fanned them out, and asked the prisoner to take one. "Don't let me see it. Just look at it and put it back. And each time I ask, 'Is this your card?' say no."

The prisoner followed instructions. After he'd put back the card he had chosen, Nard shuffled again, then, one by one, held up each card, asking, "Did you take the four of diamonds? The king of hearts? The eight of spades? And so on through all ten. To each question the prisoner answered no. But when he was asked if he'd taken the eight of spades, the pens of the polygraph rose to jagged peaks an inch high, then slowly fell.

Nard explained to the spectators that the prisoner's reactions were normal. To the prisoner he said, "You took the eight of spades, right?" The prisoner nodded.

Nard repeated the card test several times, each time showing the prisoner his very definite response when he lied. He followed these tests with a series of other questions, some nonsensitive, such as "Is your name——?" or "Do you live in Cook County?" and others, bearing on the crime. Each time he asked, "Did you kill—— (name of victim)?" the pens charting the graph shot up, indicating the same guilty response as in the card test.

An hour passed as Nard continued these tests, over and over, hoping eventually to get a normal record that might at least postpone the execution. But it was no use. The condemned man's blood pressure and breathing, recorded on the graph, continued to corroborate the verdict of the jury.

Finally, with heavy heart, Nard telephoned Governor Horner. "On the basis of my findings," he reported, "the prisoner is guilty." At 12:05 a.m., the condemned man was taken to the death chamber, strapped into the electric chair, and executed.

When the news came, his sister and mother were so hysterical that a doctor had to be called. Later, the sister, whose begging and cajoling, had dragged Nard into the case at the last minute, turned all her frustration and bitterness against him, as though he, and he alone, was to blame. At intervals over the next twelve years, she wrote to Nard, predicting he would be punished, would become paralyzed, wouldn't be able to move or speak. Nard went to authorities to try to have the letters stopped, but they claimed they could do nothing. So, month after month, year after year, the sinister predictions kept coming. And Nard, against his will, against the advice of friends, kept reading them. Gradually, his blood pressure began to climb.

The day after the execution, the story appeared in the Berkeley *Daily Gazette* and in newspapers in Oakland and San Francisco. Father, adamantly opposed to capital punishment, was deeply disturbed. The following day, he and our stepmother went to see Merodine and her three young daughters, then living in Berkeley. As they left Merodine's house, father turned to wave goodbye. He lost his balance and fell, breaking his hip. He was taken to a hospital in San Francisco, where Uncle Sterling operated on him. By summer he seemed to be recovering well. He was just starting to walk again when unexpectedly he had a heart attack, and died.

His death was a great blow. Although often excitable and overly strict, father was a man with rare insight and vision. An idealist, he wanted to make the world a better place for everyone. And he had great dreams for himself and his children.

Nard, in his way, tried to live up to those dreams.

The Boy Who Could "Hear" Through His Wrist

By 1938 the Depression had about hit bottom. World War II loomed. In February, the McDonalds invited Nard and Kay on a two-month cruise of the Caribbean. Among the islands they visited on the *Mizpah* were Haiti, Trinidad, and the Dominican Republic. They also explored waterways of Dutch Guiana, spending part of the time with natives in their dugouts. "We made two thousand feet of colored movies," Nard reported proudly.

His friendship with Eugene McDonald was not only social. The two men had much in common. Both were adventurous and inventive. In addition to being president of a great corporation, the ruggedly handsome Commander McDonald had a famous gun collection, which included a machine gun used in the St. Valentine's Day Massacre. He'd been on Arctic explorations and had received wide publicity in 1930, when he'd discovered a German colony living "back to nature" on one of the Galapagos Islands.

Fascinated by the lie detector and the variety of cases Nard had solved with it, the commander engaged him to work both for himself personally and for Zenith over a period of years spanning World War II.

They also collaborated on an experiment. With his intense interest in radio, television (still embryonic then), and all means of communication, the commander was understandably attracted to the early scientific experiments in telepathy. In 1924, he conducted what he believed was the first test made over radio to

119

Nard, left, with Eugene F. McDonald.

find evidence as to whether telepathy actually existed. In 1937, with Nard's assistance, he conducted further radio experiments, this time over a coast-to-coast network. Each broadcast included a talk on some subject, such as the skepticism of the public toward anything new, followed by actual tests. "Senders," selected from psychology classes at Northwestern University and supervised by two professors, would "beam" telepathic communications to listeners in the radio audience. Those who "received" them were to write immediately to the Zenith Foundation, reporting what they had picked up. A large statistical organization was employed to check and double-check the letters and postcards sent in.

One of the first lie detector cases Nard worked on for the commander had to do with his yacht. Approximately nine bottles of liquor and perfume valued at around $500 had disappeared from the *Mizpah*. Learning this one June, Commander McDonald asked Nard to give a lie test to a steward who had spent the winter on the yacht. Before the test the steward admitted taking one bottle of Scotch and consuming small amounts of liquor, but no more. However, his first polygram told a different story. During the second test, the steward watched the cavorting needles. Afterward he confessed to taking four additional bottles of Scotch, thirty cans of food, a dozen towels, a few gallons of gasoline, and three or four quarts of oil. When he affirmed that he had *not* stolen the $500 worth of perfume, the polygraph backed him up.

Another case Nard investigated for the commander concerned a self-proclaimed doctor, who had invented a device to convert radiant energy from the atmosphere into usable electricity. This "doctor" was going about the country demonstrating his device to individuals and heads of large corporations such as General Electric and Zenith. He was also trying to raise funds to finance his invention.

When Commander McDonald learned he was using Zenith's name in connection with his fund-raising activities, he sent Nard and several of the Zenith staff to the doctor's home in Utah to investigate. In this case Nard did not use the lie detector. After making two flights to Salt Lake City, talking with the doctor, attending lecture demonstrations of his radiant-energy device, and studying the machine as minutely as the doctor would permit, Nard wrote a detailed scientific report for Commander McDonald. His conclusion was:

> From Dr. Moray's geneal behavior in our presence, it is my opinion that he fits into the class of many well-known confidence game men whose methods and behavior I have observed ... Of course, the fact that his brother was a bank robber and murderer cannot be used against him ... It is a great regret to me that we were unable, due to the fact that he would not demonstrate further to us, to conclusively ascertain the source of his energy.

The "doctor" was informed under no circumstances to use the name of Zenith again.

In more than twenty years of lie-detecting, Nard had become used to dramatic and unusual cases. But in May 1945 Commander McDonald sent him one of the strangest. The subject was a seventeen-year-old boy, Harry Rosenberg Scott, who claimed he was totally deaf but could hear through a Zenith bone conduction hearing aid strapped like a watch to his wrist.

On the advice of a Zenith salesman, Harry, who lived in New York City, had called on the manager of the Zenith hearing aid division there regarding a job. The salesman had told him that deaf people were being hired for war work at the Chicago office.

Explaining he was stone deaf, the boy showed the manager the Zenith hearing aid on his wrist. He was a patient of Dr. Grossman's, he said, who had been exhibiting him to doctors and medical groups, including the Otolaryngology Section of the New York Academy of Medicine and the American Acoustical Society.

The amazed manager wrote immediately to Commander McDonald about this case. The commander was fascinated. Was it possible, he wondered, for the deaf to "hear" through their wrists? He envisioned a vast new market—Zenith bone conduction wrist-aids for the deaf?

Since his chief engineer was soon traveling to New York on business, the commander asked him to look up Harry Scott. But before this meeting could take place, Harry appeared at Zenith headquarters in Chicago to apply for a war job. He was taken to Commander McDonald's office, where the commander talked with him at some length.

Harry explained he'd had difficulty hearing and, in January 1944, had consulted Dr. Grossman, who told him he had progressive nerve deafness and would probably be stone deaf within a year. The preceding fall, he claimed, he had become totally deaf, and Dr. Grossman had advised him to use a bone conduction hearing aid, either held in his hand or strapped on his wrist. Dr. Grossman was so interested in his ability to hear through his wrist, Harry said, that he had taken him around exhibiting him to other doctors.

The commander telephoned Dr. Grossman in New York City. Yes, the doctor assured him, everything Harry had told him was true.

The commander then wanted to know whether Harry could actually hear through his wrist or whether he'd learned to interpret the vibrations of the bone conduction hearing aid on his wrist. Since last December when he'd bought the hearing aid, Harry replied, he'd learned to interpret vibrations into sounds and words. He couldn't hear at all through his ears.

But the boy spoke so naturally that Commander McDonald felt certain he was faking. It was impossible, he believed, for

anyone to learn to interpret vibrations through the wrist or hand
so accurately in only five months. Furthermore, standard hearing
tests indicated Harry could hear, though he still refused to admit
it.

At this point, the commander decided to send the boy to Nard
for a lie detector test.

Nard talked awhile with Harry, then asked him to take off
the hearing aid and attached him to the polygraph. He began
with questions like these: "Is your name Harry? Do you live in
New York? Have you ever stolen any money?" In another series,
still without the hearing aid, Nard asked loaded questions interspersed with nonsensitive ones: "Did you ever cheat on an examination at school? Did you eat today? Did you ever kill anyone? Are
you just a plain faker? Is your mother living? Are you faking your
deafness?" In yet another series, Nard asked: "Did Dr. Grossman
help you in your fake? Are you deliberately faking your deafness?
Do you think you're a psychopath?"

Then Nard had the boy hold the bone vibrator unit of the
hearing aid between his fingers. During this period Harry said he
could interpret sound waves readily. Following are Nard's questions and the boy's answers:

Q. Is your name Scott?

A. Yes.

Q. Are you faking?

A. I don't know.

Q. Did you have something to eat today?

A. Yes.

Q. Are you in love?

A. No.

Q. Are you deliberately faking?

A. No.

Q. Have you had breakfast today?

A. Yes.

Q. Have you lied to me during this test?

A. No.

Q. Do you know you can really hear?

A. No.

Nard's report on these tests was as follows:

> When the hearing aid was used, the subject readily answered the questions. When it was removed from his wrist or fingers, he made no verbal response.
>
> The subject's reactions—his blood pressure, pulse, respiration were specific and sometimes exceedingly marked when he was asked certain pertinent questions or when challenging or accusing statements were made to him.
>
> In his control tests when he claimed to be interpreting sound with the use of the hearing aid, in tests when the hearing aid wasn't used and the subject's back was to the examiner so that he wasn't able to resort to lip reading (he proved to be an excellent lip reader), and in particular when he was asked questions about cheating on examinations, being in love and when accusing statements were made, marked changes in his blood pressure were recorded. To these same questions he inhibited his respiratory movements (which is usual when subjects try to control their autonomic responses).

Without the hearing aid attached, Harry was observed through a one-way mirror. When a loud buzzer was sounded behind him, he made no movements, and showed no changes in his facial expression. Yet the polygraph indicated marked reactions in blood pressure, respiration, and the electrodermal phenomena to unexpected loud sounds, such as the buzzer, a clap of hands, or a loud whistle, indicating that he did perceive these sounds, although he denied hearing them.

In another common test, Nard inserted the ear nibs of a stethoscope into Harry's ears and asked him to read from a page in a book. At the same time Nard talked into the bell of the stethoscope. As Nard's voice interfered, Harry's reading voice became louder and louder, and when Nard stopped talking, Harry's voice dropped to its previous volume. Nard repeated this test four times. During the last test, Harry apparently became aware of his increased volume and overcompensated by dropping his voice almost to a whisper.

Finally, Nard showed Harry the polygrams and explained the various curves, which showed, he said, that he was faking his deafness. Harry's response was, "Maybe I'm crazy." He then said that for some psychological reason he might have confused his auditory with his tactile sense.

With this cue, Nard decided to try to transfer the subject's tactile senses back to his auditory. Again he placed the stethoscope nibs in Harry's ears and instructed him to watch his (Nard's) lips as he spoke into the stethoscope. Then Nard told him to close his eyes and try to perceive speech through his auditory mechanism. After four or five repetitions, when Nard spoke the boy's name into the bell of the stethoscope, Harry cried excitedly, "I heard you! You called my name!"

Nard smiled. "You see, you really can hear."

Within the next ten minutes, Harry said his hearing was completely restored—that he could hear even a whisper. He acted overjoyed, removed the hearing aid, tossed it on the table, and exlaimed, "Nuts to that! I won't have to be bothered with it anymore."

Admitting to this recovery, but still insisting that his problem was psychological and that he wasn't pretending, Harry was re-attached to the lie detector. In this last test Nard asked him the following questions:

Q. Is your name Harry Scott?

A. Yes.

Q. Do you hear all right now?

A. Yes.

Q. Were you faking deafness?

A. No.

Q. Have you had something to eat today?

A. Yes.

Q. Are you in love?

A. I was.

Q. Did you lie to the New York doctors about your deafness?

A. No.

Q. Is your mother living?

A. Yes.

Q. Did you fake your deafness?

A. No.

Harry reacted specifically to questions about having faked his deafness and about having lied to physicians. Nard then informed him that these results indicated that he'd been consciously malingering, and that he had been aware of it all through his period of "deafness."

Harry made no further admissions. Two days later, however, in a complete confession to Commander McDonald, he admitted he'd been fooling the world.

The hoax had started during a brief period in the Marine Reserves. The men were being given hearing tests and were asked to write down words they heard. When Harry missed some of the words, the examiner advised him to consult a doctor. So he went to Dr. Grossman. When his superiors were informed of the doctor's prognosis—that he had progressive nerve deafness and would be totally deaf within a year—he was discharged for deafness.

Harry admitted to Commander McDonald that he'd fooled not only Dr. Grossman but also his parents, who had paid for three months of lip-reading lessons. He'd paid Dr. Grossman his regular fee until the doctor had him use the bone conduction instrument on his wrist and started exhibiting him to other doctors.

Yes, he'd been lying, he confessed, and getting in deeper and deeper, and it was a big relief to get it all off his chest. He promised the commander that he would never again deceive anyone about his ability to hear. He wasn't deaf and never had been!

The commander offered to pay Harry's railroad fare to Chicago and back and advised him to go home to his family. But

Harry had other ideas. He wanted to prove that he really wasn't as deceitful as his recent behavior had indicated. And he still wanted to work for Zenith.

The commander grinned. This strange case had intrigued him. "We'll have a job for you," he promised. "You can start to work Monday morning."

CHAPTER 18

The Silent
Mass Murderer

Mass murders create excitement and publicity. But some, perhaps more than the public realizes, are quiet, sinister, often undetected — murders by poisoning. One dramatic case of Nard's appeared to be in this category.

Lilly Winter, seventy-six, a white-haired woman with a deeply lined, weatherbeaten face, lived on a twenty-acre farm some five miles from the prairie town of Fairfield, Illinois. Lilly's husband, Bert, had died some years previously. A bachelor brother, Olin, also a farmer, was gone too. Along with other relatives who'd settled the land with them and several neighbors, they were buried in a little cemetery down the road. Jean, Lilly's granddaughter, whom she'd raised since babyhood, lived with her with her three-year-old son, Donnie. Since Jean's husband was usually away in the army, only Grandma Lilly, Jean, and little Donnie were at the farm together.

One June night in 1946, Jean drove home from Fairfield, where she worked as a waitress, arriving at the farmhouse around eleven. She found her grandmother fully dressed, asleep on the bed next to Donnie. She'd probably been listening to his prayers and had dropped off, Jean figured; Lilly was a religious woman. She kissed Donnie, went to her room and tumbled into bed.

The next morning she awakened around noon. Her grandmother, who took most of the care of Donnie, called from the kitchen, "I don't know what's gotten into this boy. He wouldn't eat his dinner last night, and now he won't eat his lunch." Jean thought little of it. Donnie was a normal, healthy child. She

finished dressing, went into the kitchen, and started to fix breakfast, when Lilly cried, "Laws, will you look at that baby! He's
turning blue!"

Jean rushed to the child in terror. He was having a convul-
sion. She wrapped him in a blanket. There was no telephone on
the farm. "I'm taking him to Dr. Ransome in Fairfield," she told
her grandmother.

"You can't do that," the old lady protested. "He wouldn't last
the trip. You go by yourself and bring the doctor here."

Jean drove as fast as she dared. In Fairfield, Dr. Ransome
said he'd be out to the farm in an hour. When she returned home,
Jean found Donnie limp and gasping. She called to a farm boy to
get old Dr. Frankel, retired for many years, who lived nearby.
"And hurry!"

Dr. Frankel arrived in minutes. But he was too late. Donnie
was dead.

Since no doctor was present at the death, an autopsy was
required. It was performed at the county coroner's. The consulting chemist found 4.5 grains of arsenic in Donnie's stomach.

The state's attorney was then brought into the case. He did
not believe Jean's story. She was young and attractive; her
husband was absent most of the time. There must be another
man, he reasoned. Little Donnie must have been in the way.

Confronted with his suspicions, Jean denied her guilt repeatedly and cried hysterically, "If you don't believe me, take me
to Chicago — to Leonarde Keeler, the lie detector expert. He'll
prove I'm telling the truth."

The state's attorney made an appointment with Nard and
took Jean to his office a few days later. Nard knew only that she
was suspected of poisoning her child. As he connected her to the
polygraph, she seemed extremely nervous and apprehensive. Her
polygrams were erratic, but she didn't react suspiciously to
questions regarding the child's death. From her graphs, Nard was
convinced she'd loved Donnie and was sincerely grief-stricken.
He wanted to know about other members of her household, and
asked to test the grandmother.

Several days later they were back. The white-haired lady,
dressed in mourning for Donnie told Nard how hard her widow's
life had been . . . cooking, cleaning, milking the cow, even working in the fields. She displayed her work-hardened hands. De-

scribing Donnie's last hours, she said that when he wouldn't eat dinner, she'd given him a glass of milk and put him to bed. The next day, when he refused lunch, she'd gotten him to eat a bologna sandwich. That's when the convulsions had started. Sadly, she shook her head: "I loved him like my very own."

Nard prepared her for the test. After pumping up the cuff on her arm, he saw with shock that her blood pressure was dangerously high. Did he dare run her on the polygraph? He decided to give her just one test. Slowly, quietly, he questioned her on the death of the little boy. The only other sound was the swish of the pens on the moving paper. Her graph was even, with no specific reactions in either her blood pressure or her respiration. Yet Nard was far from satisfied. There was something strange, sinister about this woman, as if she might be holding back information. Could her abnormally high blood pressure indicate some deep, sustained guilt?

Nard urged the state's attorney to make a thorough investigation of this woman.

What the investigation turned up was spine-chilling. The attorney learned that Lilly's bachelor brother, Olin, had died mysteriously, after an hour's illness. He had lived on a two-hundred-acre farm given to him by his parents in payment of a debt. It was understood that at Olin's death, his holdings would be divided among the family. Lilly had asked him to come and live with her and Bert. When he refused, they moved in with him. Lilly took care of him and did all the cooking, cleaning, laundry, even some farm work — for fifteen years, she claimed. In return for her services, Olin promised to leave her his property.

A number of times he'd consulted a lawyer about a will, but he never got around to making it. Then, at sixty-seven, he acquired a lady friend. He told Lilly he was thinking of marrying her and leaving her part of his property. A few days later, Olin suddenly became very sick and died. Although there was a lawsuit, Lilly didn't inherit a thing; other relatives managed to get it all.

Lilly and Bert then moved back to their own house. Their daughter, Mary (Jean's mother), her husband, George, and their two daughters, Jean and Mary Anne, had been staying there in their absence. By this time, Jean, the eldest granddaughter, was married. Her husband and little Donnie lived there, too.

They'd all been together for only a short time when Lilly persuaded her husband, Bert, to draw up a joint tenancy of their property. Soon after he had signed the papers, Bert became violently ill and died—from a heart attack, according to the doctor.

Lilly became the sole owner of the farm. Then she and her daughter, Mary, had a falling out. Mary, George, and their younger daughter, Mary Anne, moved out. Jean's husband was gone most of the time by then, leaving Jean and Donnie alone with Grandma Lilly.

Sudden deaths in Lilly's past were investigated, too. Neighbors remembered that her sister had died after a two-day illness. Bert's parents had succumbed within a couple of days of each other. And there were neighbors Lilly had cared for during their last illnesses . . .

As more and more evidence of foul play came to light, Nard recommended exhuming the bodies of six relatives who had died in recent years and were buried in the cemetery near Lilly's farm. The coroner found traces of arsenic in three of these bodies.

Nothing was done about these apparent poisonings, but Lilly was taken into custody for the murder of her great-grandson. The farmhouse was searched for arsenic, but none was found. A date was set for her trial for the murder of little Donnie.

Some of Lilly's relatives and neighbors rallied to her support. Others were not so sure about her innocence. The state's attorney was puzzled. She might have had a motive for killing her parents-in-law, brother, sister, husband—to get control of the family property. But why kill little Donnie? Then a neighbor remembered that Lilly had complained, "It's just too much! I not only do all the housework and some of the farm work, but on top of all this I have to take care of Jean's baby!"

At the trial the prosecutor asked for a verdict of guilty, but not for the death penalty. But after all the witnesses had testified and the prosecuting and defense attorneys had made their pleas, to almost everyone's surprise and horror, the jury brought in their verdict—not guilty.

Lilly's farmhouse was boarded up. Jean went to live with her husband's parents, and Lilly with her estranged daughter, Mary, her husband, George, and their sixteen-year-old daughter, Mary Anne. George warned his wife to watch Granny carefully—to keep her out of the kitchen, away from food. But, apparently, Mary was not vigilant enough. After drinking from a bottle of milk, she and Mary Anne both became desperately ill. The doctor who was called took tests immediately, found arsenic in their stomachs, and was able to save their lives.

George insisted that the old lady again be arrested and tried for murder and attempted murder. While Lilly awaited her second trial in jail, her farmhouse was searched again, this time from cellar to roof. An insecticide containing arsenic was found in the attic. Lilly's prospects for another acquittal looked bleak indeed. But to Nard's amazement, at this second trial, with all the circumstantial evidence and accusations by her own daughter and granddaughters, the verdict again was not guilty.

Nard never learned what happened to Grandma Lilly after that. But he hoped that at least she was safely confined, where she could no longer pour arsenic into the food of her relatives and neighbors.

CHAPTER 19

The Crime Lab
Is Sold: Nard
and Kay Open
Separate Offices

A big change came into Nard's life in the summer of 1938. He summed it up in this answer to a query from an Ohio attorney, who had heard rumors of a change in the setup at the crime lab:

Yes, the rumors, sadly enough, are true. Apparently the yearly overhead in maintaining the Scientific Crime Detection Laboratory was a little too much for Dean Green's Law School. His budget this year was cut ... so our Laboratory and the Air Law Institute 'went by the boards.' At this critical time, the City of Chicago stepped in and purchased the Laboratory (for the police department). Charlie Wilson and Fred Inbau are staying with it for the time being. At the end of this year Inbau will join the University faculty, leaving Wilson in charge of the Crime Detection Laboratory.

I was supposed to stay on the Law School faculty at the university full time, but because I was guaranteed only a year's appointment, I decided, to remain with Northwestern half time and to open my private offices, for consulting work in personnel and criminal investigations, the other half time.

Mrs. Keeler has also opened her private offices and now has three girls assisting her.

Soon after Kay opened her office, the Chicago Sunday and daily *Herald and Examiner* launched a series of articles recounting the thrilling exploits of the "terror of killers," crime fighter Katherine Keeler. The articles told how, at the Northwestern crime lab, she'd been responsible for the solutions of hundreds of crimes beneath the "prying eye of her camera" or the "searching lens of her microscope," how she had "braved rifles of Kentucky mountaineers to secure evidence that broke up a million-dollar mail-order swindle," and "faced down fighting miners to produce in court two little pieces of tape and scientific testimony that convicted the perpetrators of a ghastly coal-mine bombing." Her new office was "the most modern private laboratory in the country," with an all-woman "crime team" — Jane Wilson, Viola (Olie) Stevens, and Edna Howse — who were all "experts," while Kay herself was "the world's greatest living authority on disputed documents — with the possible exception of her teacher, Albert S. Osborn, founder of the modern science of analyzing disputed documents and author of the most authoritative book on the subject, 'Questioned Documents.'"

In her own right, Kay was now a celebrity, with all the work

The women in the case ... They are Mrs. Katherine Keeler (right) of Northwestern University's scientific crime detection laboratory and her staff, Jane Wilson, Edna Howse and Viola Stevens (left to right). A series of articles revealing Mrs. Keeler's amazing crime-fighting exploits starts in Sunday's Herald and Examiner.

she could handle. She was making far more money than she and Nard had previously earned together.

Nard had always supported Kay's ambitions. He was proud of her keen mind and achievements. But her sudden success must have seemed overwhelming; in a sense, she had become a rival. His own situation was less definite. He had not yet opened his own office, although he definitely planned to. And he had some qualms. Could he be successful with the police crime lab now handling all the criminal cases in Chicago? Would he have to concentrate solely on personnel screening, divorce cases, and that sort of thing?

Another, more personal change had to do with a new baby of Charlie and Jane's. Jane's father had recently died and her mother had come to live with them, taking care of the baby boy, Mike, while Charlie and Jane were at work. Having no children of his own, Nard became devoted to Mike, fussing over him and playing with him as though he was his own child. During this time Nard, Charlie, and Jane became increasingly close. Kay was often with them, too, but she was making new friends now. More and more, she went her way and Nard his.

But he was too full of ideas and ambition to brood over feelings of loss. With the help of Burt Massee, he formed a corporation, Leonarde Keeler, Inc., and opened offices designed specifically for his unique business, at 124 South LaSalle Street — three blocks from Kay's office.

On November 8, 1938, Nard wrote to his old friend Elwood (Doc) Woolsey, one of the "three musketeers" from boyhood, now a bona fide M.D. working at the San Francisco Department of Public Health:

> . . . I have been in a constant turmoil, busily engaged opening my own offices and laboratory in downtown Chicago. My mornings are spent at the university, and the other half of my time in private consulting work in my own offices.
>
> I have been amazed at the amount of case work that has come in during the last two months, and I already can see that it would be impossible for me to handle this business alone. We are making polygraph tests for department stores and many other stores, banks, insurance companies, and out-of-town police departments.

I already have approximately 200 subjects scheduled to be examined this month.

There are two reputable business groups in the city who are endeavoring to finance me and organize a corporation for personnel work throughout the United States. This will necessitate the opening of branch offices in many of the larger cities. My greatest difficulty will be in obtaining men with the proper background to serve as operators, and I am also sure that a medical advisor should be on our staff.

Now, the last time I talked to you, you had no definite plans for the future ... and knowing your tendencies to delve into new and unexplored fields, I am wondering if you would be interested in joining me in this great adventure ...

I haven't heard from Heck [Ralph] Brandt [the third musketeer] since my visit with him in Los Angeles, so don't know his present status. However, just in case he is foot free, I am offering him a similar proposition to the one outlined here.

Doc wrote back and turned down this offer, saying that it had "intrigued me no end," but he had specialized for five years, and it "would be very foolish to change horses at this point."

Ralph Brandt replied in a similar vein.

On December 23, Nard wrote again to Doc, assuring him that despite his disappointment, he had anticipated Doc's thoughts and had found a fine fellow, George Smith, in the Wichita police department, who had joined forces with him.

Besides his new office, his secretary, and his new assistant polygraph examiner, Nard had a magnificent new precision-model Keeler Polygraph.

According to its manual, in June, 1938, Associated Research, Inc., the present manufacturers of the Keeler Polygraph, undertook the refinement and production of the unit.

With a background of precision manufacture of fine instruments for measurement and recording, the mechanical portions of the machine were greatly improved. As Mr. Keeler became interested in the work of Father Summers, with respect to skin resistance reaction (galvanometer), the company soon developed and added a means for measurement and recording of skin resistance change during interrogation. Through the years many improvements have raised the efficiency of the machine to its present level. Basically the original principles still form the foundation for its

Leonarde examines "subject" on lie detector.

operation. The Keeler Polygraph is the most widely used and recognized unit in the field.

Records made and filed in Keeler's office cover more than 30,000 cases. While they have never been compiled statistically, they nevertheless show a high percentage of accuracy and successful results.

This handbook is presented as a 'basic primer' to the user of the polygraph. From the basic information, any person should become

familiar with the manner of its operation. It is not intended that
the contents will do more than show the way to successful operation. Interrogation techniques must be developed or learned. The
basis of good operation lies in the development of interrogation. Up
to the present time the polygraph decribed in this manual offers
what is probably the most reliable method yet devised.

On the door to Nard's new office was inscribed: "Leonarde
Keeler, Inc., Personnel Consultants." He was referred to as a
forensic psychologist.

At the start of his new venture, Nard mostly ran polygraph
tests on job applicants and employees of various business establishments. When an employee was found deceptive about petty
thievery and confessed, Nard advised against discharging him or
her on the theory that, knowing he would be tested again in six
months, the person was unlikely to pilfer in the future.

Some subjects — say, in a business office — would give deceptive responses, but later, questioning them without the polygraph, Nard would find they had merely taken stamps, paper
clips, or other insignificant items. After "confessing", they would
run a truthful record.

This also applied when a person gave a deceptive response to
the question: "Have you ever been arrested?" He might only have
received a ticket for illegal parking. Nard learned to rephrase his
questions: "Other than paper clips, stamps, and so on, have you
ever stolen anything from your employer?" or, "Except for minor
traffic violations, have you ever been arrested?"

Other subjects gave strong deceptive reactions when their
innocence was manifest. Generally, these were sensitive, high-
strung people who had lived sheltered lives. They had guilt
complexes — believing themselves to blame for anything and
everything.

Still other sensitive people reacted strongly to certain loaded
words: *rape, burglary, sex, murder*. Just hearing the words made
them feel guilty. In testing such subjects, Nard often changed his
vocabulary to make sure it was not the particular word, rather
than the thought, that had caused a reaction. For instance, when
asked, "Did you take the money out of your boss's drawer?" the
subject might react to the word *steal* but not to the word *take*.

Beyond screening employees and job applicants, testing suspected malingerers, and investigating various irregularities in business establishments, Nard worked on other noncriminal cases, including suspected infidelity, questioned paternity, and divorce. Usually these cases were headaches; those who requested the lie tests were often psychotic. Nard used to say that when a husband brought his wife in to be tested on her fidelity, she was usually truthful and he deceptive — although not always.

Nard turned down most such cases, but when a reputable lawyer called on him to help save a marriage or reputation, he was glad to cooperate. A wealthy society woman, for instance, suspected her husband of infidelity. She didn't know whether she wanted a divorce, but she couldn't go on as things were. Her lawyer talked with her husband, who explained that it was his wife who was going through a change. She'd seen him in his car with a girl from his office whom he'd driven home several times, merely as a courtesy — she happened to live near his house. But he had no interest in her. He loved his wife, but he could no longer tolerate her suspicions.

The lawyer then suggested he take a lie detector test. The wife was surprised when her husband agreed, and she watched while Nard gave the test. Afterward Nard explained the graph to her. Finally she was convinced that her husband's infidelity had been a figment of her imagination. The husband was so relieved that he offered Nard twice his usual fee.

In another case, it was the husband who asked for a divorce. His wife, feeling that her husband had neglected her, had gone off one weekend with another woman and two men, one an old beau. The two women took a room together at a motel; the men shared another room. During the evening the two couples danced and drank late, then they all retired to their separate rooms. But the woman friend decided to go back to one of the men, leaving the "neglected" wife alone for the rest of the night. At least, that was the wife's story. The husband didn't believe it — until his lawyer suggested a lie detector test. The wife passed. She admitted she'd necked a bit, but nothing more. Her polygrams convinced the husband she was telling the truth. Once more, Nard and his polygraph saved a marriage.

Then there was the case of an eighteen-year-old college student who took a girl out riding one night and had an affair. He took precautions, but soon the girl claimed that she was pregnant and told him he had to marry her. When the boy refused, her family pressured him, and finally, he gave in to what became a dismal marriage. Forced into a situation he hated, the boy felt degraded. Shortly after the baby was born, he found some love letters from another man to his wife. These letters convinced him that his wife was having an affair, and he consulted a lawyer. First, the lawyer had blood tests taken, which proved that the baby could not possibly be the young husband's child. Then, he asked Nard to examine the girl on the lie detector. After the test, the girl confessed that her boy friend was the baby's father. When he'd refused to marry her, she'd forced the other boy into it. Thanks largely to the polygraph, the marriage was annulled and a legal guardian appointed for the baby.

CHAPTER 20

The Keelers

Nard and Kay had always greeted me with the utmost cordiality, but shortly before Christmas of the year they both opened their own offices, I saw things were not the same. I stopped over to see them on my way home to Caliofornia. Nard didn't seem happy, and my three days there were disturbing. Kay was glum. She seemed to resent me. After that, except for a brief glimpse at a railroad station in Sacramento, I didn't see Nard again for seven years.

Olie, Viola Stevens, told me that for about three years, after opening her own office, Kay was riding high in her handwriting business, working on sensational murders and suicide, bomb, extortion, and vote-fraud cases. According to one report, she became nationally celebrated for developing a technique to determine fraudulent marks on ballots and for her expert testimony in many important trials.

Of Kay's three assistants, Edna Howse left, but Jane and Olie stuck with her. Then, after a couple of years, her cases began to taper off. She spent less and less time at her office. "Kay was temperamental," Olie explained. "Friendly one day; the next you couldn't please her. She had a complex personality."

Ever since Lindbergh's widely heralded nonstop flight to Paris in 1927, there had been many famous flights—to the Hawaiian Islands, across the Pacific, around the world. On a world trip I took, we were on the lookout for Amelia Earhart, whose plane had vanished in the South Pacific in 1937.

In their Stanford days, Nard and some of his "flying" buddies had planned an expedition to the Valley of Ten Thousand Smokes

143

Katherine (Kay) Keeler, Nard's wife, exhibits ballots in vote fraud case.

in Alaska, hoping to discover tropical vegetation. Subsequently, Nard had flown on commercial planes. But cabins were not pressurized in those days, and after he began to suffer from high blood pressure, he had to give up flying altogether.

But Kay, who had first learned to fly in Hawaii, became more enthusiastic than ever. With the money from her handwriting cases, she bought her own plane—a Piper Cub—and kept it at a private field west of Chicago, where she took lessons.

Around that time, Kay met a dapper young Argentinian with a dark mustache, Rene' Dussaq. More daring than Nard had ever been, Rene' was a flyer, a deep-sea diver, and, for several years, a Hollywood stunt man. Besides smashing up cars and careening them off cliffs, he'd once leapt from one plane in flight to another. In real life, he'd fought in two Latin American revolutions, in two duels (one with swords, one with guns), and knew six languages.

Kay, with her affinity for adventure, was almost inevitably attracted to this daredevil. Whether she went out with him alone at that time, I can't say. I only know that Nard was unhappy.

Just before Christmas in 1940, news came that Nard was in the hospital. He no longer answered my letters. He seemed to have dropped out of the world. War had broken out. Hitler's Panzer divisions were rolling across Europe, devastating towns and cities. Bombs were falling on England. Tales of atrocities leaked out of Nazi concentration camps.

For years, Nard had talked about the Mayo Clinic, and during this period he traveled to Rochester, Minnesota, for intermittent examinations and treatments. But he didn't want outsiders to know about his illness, and most of the time he seemed to be in good shape.

On April 13, 1940, Nard and Kay separated. Nard moved into the Lakeshore Athletic Club, where they had been married ten years earlier, and Kay, taking Chief with her, rented an apartment on the ground floor of an old Victorian mansion on North Dearborn Parkway.

During their separation, I saw Kay briefly in San Francisco. She looked more beautiful than ever and was her old friendly self. I also felt she was still in love with Nard. Indeed, a few months later, Nard moved back with Kay in what proved an unsuccessful effort at reconciliation. This time, it was Kay who moved out. Nard remained in the North Dearborn apartment—he lived there for the rest of his life.

After the divorce, in June 1941, Kay closed her office. A short time later she married Rene' Dussaq. Olie and Jane went to work for Nard. Their secretarial skills and expertise in handwriting analysis made them a great asset. Olie, who was extremely competent and dependable, managed the office. Jane, with Nard's training, became the first woman polygraph examiner.

Despite Nard's divorce and bouts of illness and depression, his business was booming. He'd taken on still another assistant, and the three men and Jane had more cases than they could handle. The men who worked for Nard at the La Salle Street office included George Smith, George Haney, and Lester Schrieber; later, when the operation moved into larger quarters, there were others.

While his assistants handled most of the routine cases, police chiefs and law enforcement officers in other cities called Nard to work on cases that baffled the local authorities. Of these, one of the most disturbing involved an automobile accident. A prominent businessman from another city had been driving with his wife, when his car apparently swerved off the road and hurtled down a steep enbankment. The man jumped to safety, but his wife was killed.

This seeming "accident" took on new dimensions when investigators combed the area and learned the husband had recently taken out a double-indemnity insurance policy on his wife's life. After fruitlessly grilling the husband, the sheriff persuaded him to take a lie detector test. Knowing his refusal would be an indication of guilt, the husband agreed to go with two sheriff's deputies to Nard's office in Chicago where Nard ran several tests on him. Asked if he'd murdered his wife, the man appeared calm and confident but showed a definite reaction on the polygraph. Later, in a peak-of-tension test, when Nard asked questions like "Did you strangle your wife? Did you smother her? Did you hit her with a hammer?" he still seemed composed, despite the jittery movements of the polygraph pens. But when, still speaking in a quiet, even tone, Nard asked, "Did you hit her over the head with an iron pipe?" the pens zigzagged wildly. Before the test, investigators had found a piece of iron pipe at the scene of the accident. The unknowing suspect was caught completely by surprise. Nard repeated the last test. As the incriminating question passed, the husband's blood pressure dropped and he breathed deeply in relief—a classic sign of deception.

When Nard removed the blood pressure cuff, pneumograph, and galvanometer, the suspect was visibly shaken. Muttering that it wasn't necessary to question him further—they already knew the truth—he hurried out of Nard's eighth-floor office. The deputies followed, but were too slow. A window at the end of the corridor was open. The suspect climbed over the sill and jumped.

Nard stayed home in shock for several days. He knew the man was guilty. The investigators knew it. But this suicide, by a person he had just examined on the lie detector, who had not been tried by judge or jury, troubled him deeply.

But this is not to say that Nard was soft toward calloused or dangerous criminals. His first concern, always, was to protect the public. Behind his facade of calmness, understanding, compassion, he could be tough when the situation demanded it.

After opening his office, Nard received a flood of publicity. In many quarters the lie detector came under fire from those who felt it undermined basic values of honesty or threatened to become an instrument of coercion. In this letter written in August 1940, to the writer, J. P. McEvoy, who was preparing a story about his work, Nard defended the social uses of the polygraph:

I was much interested in your question, brought up yesterday in our meeting—'If the polygraph is so successful and can save companies money, why don't the chain stores make more use of it?'

I visited the comptroller of one of the big chain stores that afternoon and asked him why, after we had examined four hundred employees in Michigan and made a spot recheck, he did not continue using the technique in his business. He answered that the test was highly successful, had stopped much pilfering in their stores, and, he was sure, had prevented irregularities. He said, however, that they were not using the test any further at this time because of the public attitude.

It so happened that two women's clubs in the state of Michigan held indignation meetings when they heard that all the employees of this chain were being subjected to the lie-detector test. None of the women made any inquiry as to the technique and purpose of the test and yet condemned our operations publicly. Our work was also condemned in the editorials of two or three radical papers. The company auditor said that he would use our services throughout the country, providing the reactionary attitude of the public did not exist.

This official suggested an educational program (possibly lectures before women's and Rotary clubs), particularly in small communities where this work would be carried on. All mothers and fathers think that their sons and daughters applying for positions are honest. It should be pointed out to them that there is a large amount of dishonesty among employees and, to save sons and daughters from being tarred with the same brush, the polygraph technique should be welcome. And, sons and daughters are protected from false accusations and suspicions when the organization in which they are employed is relatively free from dishonesty.

He said also that officials of labor organizations should be approached, that it should be pointed out to them that one of the drawbacks in unionizing employees of certain concerns is protection of dishonest employees—not wage or hour regulations. According to this comptroller, it is impossible to discharge employees in many unionized groups unless absolute proof of guilt is presented. He said that there would be less resentment against unions providing it is understood between the union and the management that, when a question of individual integrity arises, the union would agree to abide by the findings of the polygraph. It would be understood that tests would be made by an outside, disinterested party. He suggested that it be pointed out to newspaper editors, women's clubs, and other community organizations that the test procedure could be of great value to the employee, building character and morale; and, at the same time the company would be saved large sums of money which could later be applied to employee salary increases.

Controversy of this type was to arise increasingly in the entire field of polygraph investigations. But at this time, Nard and his assistants had such a plethora of cases to handle that he was not overly concerned.

CHAPTER 21

Even The Nicest People Get Into Trouble

Nard's empathy and concern for people, combined with his knowledge of psychology, often made him seem more like a family counselor than a police interrogator. This was particularly true one Friday morning when he arrived at his office early to keep an appointment.

Seated in his waiting room were the pastor of a church in an outlying district of Chicago, his eldest daughter, the church treasurer, and a precinct police captain.

In Nard's private office, the captain outlined the case. The preceding Sunday a considerable amount of money had been pilfered from the church collection. There had been two worship services. Afterward, the treasurer, the financial secretary, and a committee of the elders had counted the collection money. Besides the two services there had been a special peace offering, so the total amount was larger than usual.

After telling the treasurer that his daughters would be at home to receive the money, the minister left with his wife for meetings at other churches. They returned home at about four p.m.

There were five teenage children—four daughters and a twelve-year-old son. The eldest, a rather plain girl, was the Sunday school treasurer and served on several church committees; the second oldest was the pretty one; she was to act in a play that night at the parish house.

149

The latter told her father she had let the treasurer in at two p.m., his usual time, and that he'd put the bag of collection money behind the door in her father's study, the customary place. The fifteen-year-old reported that an hour later the treasurer had returned with paper currency he'd received in exchange for coins from the morning's collection.

The remainder of that afternoon, the minister worked in his study on a religious article that he'd promised his publisher by the following day. His wife and the girls were busy preparing dinner, dressing for the play, and helping the budding actress, who, that night, was the center of attraction. They all attended the play, which received enthusiastic applause. Afterward, she was complimented on her performance.

The following morning the minister took the money bag to the bank. At the teller's window he opened it to find rolls of coins and checks, but no dollars. The teller counted the money the treasurer and the elders had listed on a deposit slip, then looked up and announced, "You're short four hundred eighty dollars!"

The minister searched the bag: Nothing. Bewildered, he took the money back and left. Outside from a phone booth, he called the treasurer, who claimed to know nothing about the loss. "I'll meet you at your house in an hour," he said.

After again counting the money and verifying the loss, the two men went through the house looking for signs of burglary. They found a partly open window, but no indication of a break-in. Deciding the money must have been left at the church, they went there to search. But again they found nothing. The following day the minister went to the precinct station and told the police captain of the loss.

Later, the captain asked the minister, the chairman of the board of elders, and several board members who they thought was guilty. Each suspected the church treasurer. A night dispatcher for a trucking firm, he was married and had two children. He was often in debt. At various times he'd borrowed money from some of the elders. He owed money on his rent. His landlord happened to be the chairman of the board of trustees.

Since the treasurer and the minister had been the last two people to handle the money, the captain suggested making an appointment for them with Leonarde Keeler for lie detector tests.

The treasurer agreed, but on one condition—that the minister's four daughters be tested also.

This created an uproar. "Unthinkable! An indignity!" the members cried. The minister, his wife, and all the elders were against it. Besides, they'd already made up their minds—the treasurer was the thief.

The minister then suggested a compromise. If the treasurer would take the test, he and his eldest daughter would also take it. This was agreeable to him.

The police captain rose. "And now, Mr. Keeler, it's up to you. The reverend, his daughter, and the treasurer are out there waiting for us. The reverend suggests you run the treasurer first. If you find him deceptive, you won't have to run the others."

But as a secretary ushered them all in, the daughter loudly insisted, "No Papa, I should be first! I'm already late for work!"

And so, after the introductions and a few moments of friendly chitchat, Nard led the daughter into one of the interrogation rooms and connected her to the lie detector. The police captain watched, unseen.

She seemed confident, almost irritable, as though she just wanted to get it all over with quickly. As he explained the procedure, Nard noticed quite a contrast between her fashionable clothes and her bleak expression. He started the chart drive motor on the polygraph and began. She gave strong reactions to the questions: "Do you know who took the collection money? Did you take it? Have you ever stolen money from the church?"

On a second test she reacted to the exact amount of money stolen.

After the test, Nard explained the peaks and dips on her polygrams. For a moment the two sat silently. Then, gently, Nard asked, "Do you want to tell me about it?"

Tears spilled down her face. Then, in a gush of words, it all came out. She was a minister's daughter—the oldest in the family. Everything had been expected of her. She worked on committees at the church, helped with the housework, took care of the younger children. Their family was so large her parents could barely pay their bills, let alone afford luxuries. She'd never had much of anything of her own.

The sister nearest her age was pretty and popular. She'd

acted in a play, and she and the other sisters all had boy friends.
She had no one. She was homely. Yes, she said, she had taken the
money. She'd been taking money for a long time—from the
Sunday school treasury and other funds she'd been given for
safekeeping. She was supposed to be so competent, so responsible.
Everybody trusted her! Then last Sunday she'd taken all the bills
from the bag of collection money.

Nard asked, "And what did you do with all the money?"

"I spent it, every cent of it, for lessons at a charm school, a
course in ballroom dancing, stylish clothes—so I'd be noticed, so
people would know I was alive!" She sobbed quietly for several
moments, then looked up. "What's going to happen now? Will I be
sent to jail?"

Smiling, Nard gave her hand a little pat. "I don't think so."

"Thank you, Mr. Keeler." Her eyes suddenly lit up, her lips
broke into a smile. "You don't know how relieved I am to have it
all out."

Nard looked at her appraisingly. "There's something *you*
don't know. You're a very attractive young woman."

The daughter agreed to pay back the money in installments.
After talking with her shocked father, Nard was assured that her
family and members of the church would help her to start a new,
constructive, happier life.

In another case, Nard helped a young man, who like the
minister's daughter was in serious trouble.

Keith Alson, a naive boy in his twenties, lived on a small
farm with his father, Charles, supervisor of a large dairy. Keith
was engaged to a pretty twenty-two-year-old girl, Frieda Borman, who lived with her parents in Gary, Indiana, an industrial
city, near Chicago. Frieda worked downtown in this city and
commuted to work on a streetcar. As often as possible, Keith
drove in to see her. Theirs was an old-fashioned romance, ap-
proved by his father and both her parents. They seemed deeply in
love.

One Sunday in November, Keith picked Frieda up at her
home and drove her out to his farm, where they spent several
hours together. Then, two days later, he arrived unexpectedly at
her parent's home. They met him at the door in a state of
agitation.

"Oh, Keith, I'm glad you've come!" her mother cried. "We've been trying to reach you."

The father added grimly, "The police want to talk to you."

"The police? What for? What's happened?"

The anguished parents explained that the day before, Frieda had gone to work as usual. A little after six that evening, a friend had seen her board a streetcar downtown, apparently to return home. But she never arrived. Her parents waited anxiously for several hours, then called the police. A search began. Hearing this news, Keith went immediately to the police department, identified himself and offered to help in the search.

Five days later Frieda's fully dressed body was found in a field near a dirt road some ten miles from the city. There were no outward signs of violence. But in the morgue, the coroner found evidence that she had been criminally attacked. No marks of any other physical violence nor any traces of poison accounted for her death.

Some two dozen people, friends, relatives, neighbors— everyone with any connection to Frieda—were called to the police station for questioning. Eight of these, including Keith and his father, were detained.

At this point Nard entered the case. The officers in charge felt certain Keith and his father were guilty. But after testing all eight suspects at the police department, Nard believed, from their polygrams, that none had committed the murder, although he suspected that Keith Alson was withholding some vital information. All the other suspects ran clear records.

When no decisive evidence was uncovered, either from the polygraph tests or by other means, Frieda was finally buried and the case closed.

Then, some four months later, the police department set up a special homicide squad. Two ambitious young officers in this unit delved into the all-but-forgotten case of Frieda Borman. Believing Keith Alson definitely involved, they managed to locate the car that had belonged to him at the time of Frieda's death, which had since been repossessed by the finance company. In it, they found evidence, reaffirmed by chemical tests, that convinced them a woman had been criminally attacked in the car.

Their evidence was sent to the FBI. Keith and Charles Alson were arrested, charged with the rape and murder of Frieda

Borman, and jailed. The police believed Keith had committed the crime alone, but that his father had become an accessory by trying to protect his son.

Frieda's body was exhumed and new chemical tests made. But still the experts could not ascertain the cause of her death.

Although Nard had found the Alsons truthful, the police were not convinced. Day after day, they grilled the two men. Once, when Keith and his father were left alone, a transcript was made of their conversation. Following are excerpts:

Keith. Did you make that statement?

Father. I made that statement . . . I wanted to help you. I haven't told nothing but the truth all the way through. They wanted to know what the show was that night. You know I can't remember shows. Every show I ever go to I fall asleep. Remember that time you came over and got me and we went to the Tivoli? What was that show? "Always in Trouble . . . Always in Trouble". That's one show I'll always remember. Yesterday, I was trying to think of that show, and do you know, I couldn't think of it?

Keith. Before they had me locked up, they were questioning me day and night, night and day, so that I couldn't remember stuff . . . yesterday they said I remembered it too well. *(pause)* You shouldn't have made that statement.

Father. No, I suppose it didn't sound good. They kept hounding me . . . hounding me . . . I didn't know what to do. I told them I'd make a statement, that I'd sign it as the truth, but that I was making a false statement . . . My God, my God, I hope they get the culprit. They want me to come clean. Well, my land, when I wasn't out there how could I come clean?

Keith. Did they take you out there, too?

Father. Yes, they took me out there. They wanted to know if that was the exact spot. I said, "My God, boys, how do I know? I was never out there." I don't know that road . . . If I was to die the next minute, I couldn't go out there today . . . and they ask if that's the exact spot!

Keith. What was in that statement the other night?

Father. That what's-his-name ... he wanted to know ... My God, I just wanted to call him the biggest Dog-damn liar in the world, but of course I didn't ... He continually accused me of having intercourse with that poor girl. If she could come right in that door and face me this very minute, could she ever say that I in any way mistreated her? The girl that I expected to be my daughter-in-law? Why, it's unthinkable ... God knows, I'll help them to do everything I can to still solve it ... I expect this will always stand against me ... but I'm fifty-two years old ... my life's been spent. I sure had the hardships. But your life's just begun. I'd be willing to take anything that had to be done.

Keith. Haven't had any peace of mind ...

Father. I've worked and worked ... every day of the week- ... from early morning to late in the evening. Go home, grab a bit of supper, and run back to finish up. Now, if I'd done anything like that, would I have stayed around there? I had nothing to fear when I left there ...

Keith. They used the lie detector on me, too.

Father. I answered questions truthfully. I don't know. I hope that everything comes out good.

After studying the transcript, the two officers of the homicide squad who had reopened the case began to have some doubts. They called Nard to discuss the case. He told them that he was still convinced the father and son were innocent, and urged them to search for other suspects.

Several weeks later, the officers brought a new suspect to Nard's Chicago office, Henry Schurg—his age was around thirty. He lived near Frieda's home.

During his preliminary interview, Nard learned that Henry was married and had two children. He dressed neatly. There was nothing strange or abnormal about him—just an ordinary guy.

But his polygrams told a different story. Nard made several tests. Each showed deception. He'd lied on most of the questions. Nard urged him to talk. Finally, Henry admitted having sex relations with young girls and children in his neighborhood. Asked if Frieda had been one of those girls, he said, no. When

Nard continued to probe, Henry stopped him abruptly. "Okay, okay! I'll give it to you straight. Here's exactly what happened."

Around seven o'clock on the night Frieda disappeared, Henry was driving home when he saw her get off the streetcar and start walking home. He pulled up alongside her. "Hi, there! Can I give you a lift?" She recognized him and got in his car. She'd worked late. She was tired. Henry suggested they take a little ride, saying that it would do her good to get some fresh air. No, she protested. She had to get home. She was already late. Her parents would worry.

Pretending not to hear, he drove faster, out toward the country, then turned off onto a dirt road where there was hardly any traffic. As he drove he made passes at her with his free hand. She pulled away, crying, "Stop it! Take your hand off me!" He kept on driving, bumping over potholes. "You take me right home, do you hear? I hardly know you. I don't want to have anything to do with you."

"Okay, okay, if that's how you feel, you can damn well get out of this car and go home by yourself." He slowed down. Frieda flung open the car door, jumped out, and started running breathlessly across a field. Trying to take off her coat, she tripped and fell on her back. Henry stopped the car, jumped out, and in moments was on top of her, pulling up her dress. For an instant she struggled. Her eyes stared up at him in terror. Then, suddenly, she went limp. She'd had a heart attack —from fright, Henry figured. He patted her face, trying to bring her to, then gave her artificial respiration. When he knew he couldn't revive her, that she was dead, he walked back to his car.

Reaching home, he found the belt from her coat in his car. The next day he took it out to the field where he'd left her and dropped it there. He didn't see her body. He didn't want to see it, he told Nard.

After his confession, the police officers who had been watching the tests took Henry into custody. Meantime, the officers brought Keith and Charles Alson to Nard's office for additional tests. the father's record was clear. He explained that his only part in the case had been to try to help his son. But on one of Keith's tests, when Nard asked, "Have you ever raped a girl?", the boy stuttered, "N-n-no . . . Y-yes." The polygraph pens wobbled eratically.

At the end of the test, Keith explained why he had stuttered and why, on his first tests, he'd shown deceptive reactions. He'd been very much in love with Frieda and had great respect for her. Then, the day before her disappearance, he'd taken her out to his farm. They'd become passionate . . . lost control. They made love. Although both had religious backgrounds, Keith didn't think they had really done wrong, for they planned soon to be married. But when he learned of her disappearance, then of her death in a reported rape-slaying, he panicked.

The charges against Keith and his father were dropped. The lie detector had helped to save another innocent young man from a possible life term, and his father, who had stood behind him, from a long incarceration.

CHAPTER 22

After Pearl Harbor

After Pearl Harbor, America quickly geared for the war it had entered at last. Millions of men were drafted or enlisted. War plants stepped up their production. Shipyards hummed. The Depression was over.

Women took over many jobs formerly held by men. I worked in a Sacramento radio station, broadcasting news and a daily home-front program urging listeners to buy war bonds, volunteer for the Red Cross, serve as airplane spotters, work in canneries, join the various women's auxiliaries of the armed forces, and so on.

In Chicago, Nard's assistants were enlisting. Kay and Rene Dussaq moved to Washington, D.C. Soon Rene joined the parachute ski patrol, and Kay the Women's Auxiliary Service Pilots (WASP). About a thousand women fliers were in that special auxiliary. They ferried war planes from factories to airfields, towed targets to be shot at, and engaged in other demanding and dangerous missions within the United States.

Nard, who was thirty-eight at this time, was eager to enlist in the army. He made this clear in a letter to a friend, Captain James Delaney, at Wright Flying Field, Dayton, Ohio:

I suppose by this time you have been informed of the bad news regarding the outcome of my examination . . .

I was told by my family physician that there wasn't a chance for me to get into the service with my heart history . . . When it came to my blood pressure, it was found to be 180 systolic over 100 diastolic. As far as I know, this is the only real defect that would make me ineligible . . .

... the opening that you and Al had for me I consider one of the important ones in the intelligence work in the country, and I'd give a whale of a lot to be able to step in and really do a job. As a matter of fact, I'm being a very circumspect sort of a guy these days, and am going to make a rather thorough study into my blood pressure situation and by hook or crook stabilize it some way so that I may, in the future, pass another examination. It's either that or obtaining a waiver on my physical condition, which I presume is almost an impossibility.

Golly, Jim, you don't know how disappointed I am ...

A second letter to Jim Delaney showed Nard's renewed determination:

A few weeks ago I discovered a preliminary report on some experimental work done on hypertensive dogs at the Medical School of the University of Illinois. Apparently all the hypertensive dogs they treated with enormous doses of Vitamin A had completely recovered. I followed this up with the head of the Physiology Department and have been elected as their first human guinea pig. My treatment will start in approximately two weeks, as soon as they obtain the necessary supply. The ordinary Vitamin A capsule that one buys in a drugstore is 15,000 units and I'll be taking approximately one million units by mouth per day. The dogs gained their normal blood pressure level in from two to three weeks after beginning treatment. So you can't tell—might hear me barking any time.

But like all the remedies and diets Nard tried, the one million units per day of Vitamin A apparently had little, if any, effect. As it was, Nard eventually worked on many cases for the army.

Meanwhile, he busied himself with plans for a mobile crime detection laboratory. About the "Illinois State Police Mobile Crime Detection Laboratory and Emergency Unit," in an article for the October 1942 *Illinois Police Journal,* Nard wrote:

The Illinois State Police Department is now operating a new 60-mile-an-hour mobile unit with which it can bring assistance to any community within the state in time of riot, crime, flood, conflagration, or other emergency.

It is almost a complete crime detection laboratory on wheels; a

Mobile Crime Lab.

rolling police department with better equipment than the majority of departments in the country; a mobile hospital where two major operations can be performed simultaneously; a combat unit tough enough to handle anything short of an army tank; an emergency electric power station, radio transmitter, fire-fighting and life-saving unit; in general, a complete emergency outfit designed to bring the finest in crime detection, law enforcement, and life-saving facilities to any part of the state on a few hours notice.

The unit was first conceived by Gov. Dwight H. Green several years ago, but there was nothing he could do until after he had established the Department of Public Safety. He then conferred with Director T. P. Sullivan and with me and gave us our orders to go ahead. Our first idea was merely to have a crime detection laboratory installed in a trailer to be towed by a squad car. Then we realized that there would be much greater public benefit and economy if it included complete facilities for all types of emergencies. The result is the new mobile unit, about the size and shape of a typical highway bus.

Behind the driver's compartment is a turret of armor plate and bullet-resistant glass which can be elevated to a commanding position four feet above the roof by means of an engine-operated hydraulic hoist.

And there was much more. A separate article in that same issue of the *Police Journal* referred to T. P. Sullivan as "one of the foremost police authorities in the world," and to Nard as "the inventor of the Keeler polygraph or lie detector and an internationally famous criminologist." The two men, who had been friends for years and worked on many cases together, drew up the plans, decided on all the equipment needed, were honored at the christening ceremony, and received nationwide publicity.

Alas, the mobile unit turned out to be a dud. Too small for a crime lab or hospital, too big for a mobile unit, it was used mainly as an exhibit at fairs. But you can't win them all, and that first huge, unwieldy vehicle was a forerunner of the more compact mobile crime detection units in use today in some cities.

Also in 1942, Nard became advisory director for the Scientific Crime Detection Laboratory for the state of Illinois, a title he held for the remainder of his life, working on many cases for the state police.

And in his LaSalle Street office, as at Northwestern, he continued to train polygraph examiners—mostly police officers at first, later military and government officials. His courses were for two weeks only and, space being limited, for only a few men at a time. He knew the courses should cover many matters: the medical and psychological aspects of deception, the mechanics of the polygraph, techniques of interrogation, and polygram interpretation. But he would have to wait. Later, in 1948, when he moved to much larger quarters on Ohio Street, he expanded the courses to six weeks and brought in guest lecturers—doctors, psychologists, and various specialists. Today there are many schools for polygraph examiners, but the Keeler Polygraph Institute was the first. It is still going strong.

Nard lived an intensely keyed-up life, dealing all day with emotions—jobs, reputations, matters of life and death. Not everyone could bear up under such strain, and indeed one of his polygraph examiners, an extremely conscientious young man, had to quit. It was Nard's travel and active social life, often connected with his profession, that gave him a chance to unwind.

On his frequent trips, he'd be gone anywhere from a couple of days to a couple of weeks, carrying a portable polygraph. He'd ride on crack trains with now-nostalgic names—the Twentieth Century Limited, the Chief, El Capitan, the Burlington Zephyr.

On the train, he'd prepare the case he was to run. And after he'd run the case, studied the polygrams, discussed them with officials, and written his report, he'd come home, his sandy hair slightly rumpled—as Olie put it, "worn out from the strain of trying to get someone to tell the truth."

While still at the Northwestern crime lab, Nard was asked to participate in a nationwide effort to combat juvenile delinquency. In a letter to Lorenzo S. Buckley of Oakland, California, then chairman of the Juvenile Crime Committee of the United States Junior Chamber of Commerce, he expressed himself at length on this perennial problem:

> ... The problem is so tremendous in its complexity that, with our present attitude of government, law making, and political set-up, I see little hope in making any great advancement with the proposed Junior Association program in this city ...
>
> The two fundamental causes, of course, are heredity and environment. We can do nothing about the former after the child is born, and of the latter, the child's behavior patterns are already well organized by the time he reaches the juvenile authorities ...
>
> It seems to me that the prevalence of juvenile delinquency is a symptom of social conditions, and that to attack the problem directly is attempting to cure the cause by treating the symptom ...
>
> We so often see reports indicating the soundness of the Scout movement, Y.M.C.A. training, etc., that boys belonging to these institutions are seldom among the ranks of our court habitues. This is undoubtedly true, but in making our deductions I believe we place the cart before the horse. Boys are not taken into the scouts before the age of ten to twelve years. Those who join or remain members in good standing are boys already grounded in sound principles of life, otherwise they would not be interested in the Scout movement, or they would find themselves misfits in a highly principled environment and soon drift away, finding their own social strata in neighborhood gangs ...
>
> Newspapers, movies, radio, daily associates, families—all part of the social life—have such a greater influence on child development than schools or even playgrounds that the great problem, instead of juvenile delinquency, is social bluffing, dishonest and political selfishness, and corruption ...
>
> Gambling, vice and liquor laws are laughed at, while our city fathers reap a golden harvest. The word politician is often synony-

mous with crook, hoodlum, and grafter here as well as in most large cities. Many judges are part of the political ring and, whether Democrats or Republicans, or members of any other organization, adhere to the rules of the spoils system. And the child is just a product of this rotten system.

If the Junior Association of Commerce really wants to contribute something to society, and incidentally, help prevent juvenile delinquency, I suggest it get behind a movement to organize good government.

If need be, start a clean political machine and line up the really worthwhile of the community to buck the crooked machines. When the Association's party comes into power, then it will be easy to provide for all the necessary coordinating bodies and to establish a scientific procedure for controlling and eliminating, to a large degree, juvenile delinquency . . .

Unless we can unite the better elements of citizenry to combat lawlessness in general, particularly in municipal politics and government, I see no possibility of setting up a permanent workable plan for juvenile crime prevention.

CHAPTER 23

Murder In The Bahamas

Soon after opening his own office, Nard came to know one of the great private eyes of the day; a New York detective who always seemed more like a character in glamorous crime fiction than a real-life detective. He was Raymond C. Schindler.

White-haired, paunchy, genial in a guarded sort of way, Ray spent most evenings at expensive restaurants and nightclubs, always with a group—sometimes a group of clients, most of them wealthy and important; at other times, business associates and their wives. Usually there was a pretty girl or two along. Ray loved to dance. His nightlife was part of his way of operating, enabling him to meet key people and pick up news and gossip. In his practice, he had the reputation of charging astronomical fees, except when a client he deemed worthy was broke and badly in need of his services. In such cases, his services were free.

Ever since 1911, when he'd first used the dictagraph in his investigations, Ray had kept up with all the newest methods of scientific crime detection. He also developed unorthodox methods of his own. Once, to break down a murder suspect, he had a story printed in just one copy of a newspaper, describing hitherto unknown details of the murder, and placed it where the suspect was sure to see it.

To such an ingenious mind the lie detector had strong appeal. In one of Ray's cases, a corporation president and art collector had three of his most prized paintings, insured for large sums, stolen from his posh Manhattan hotel suite. After lining up five suspects: three hotel employees, a loyal family servant, and the corporation president himself (because of his insurance on the

165

pictures), Ray wired Nard to come immediately to New York to run all the suspects on the polygraph.

The hotel employees—a busboy, houseman, and window washer—who had been in the suite around the time the paintings disappeared, ran clear records. The corporation president's polygrams showed nervousness, but no definite deceptive reactions. The servant, who, incidentally, had been the one to inform her boss of the thefts, did not show up for the tests.

Later, this highly moral, forty-five-year-old woman confessed. She couldn't face a lie detector test—because she was the guilty person. She'd been devoted to her boss's wife and children, who were away on vacation. In their absence, she claimed, the husband had been partying and carrying on with other women. To punish him, she'd stolen his most prized possessions, the three paintings. And where were they? To her stunned interrogators she admitted, shamefaced, that she had ripped those irreplaceable masterpieces out of their frames and burned them in an incinerator.

Although Nard did not actually run this servant on the polygraph, both Ray and the corporation president agreed that Nard's presence there had broken the case. This was one of a number of cases in which the guilty subject confessed rather than submit to a test.

Another case involved a large East Coast newspaper. A line insulting the owner of the paper had been surreptitiously inserted into a classified ad column. For that one, both Ray and Nard had to do a lot of boning up on printers, presses, and typesetting. Then there was the case of the pilfering clerk in a camera shop. After his first polygraph test, the clerk admitted stealing $11,000 worth of merchandise. The second test indicated that he was withholding information. After several more tests, he finally confessed that over a certain period he had stolen around $35,000 worth of photo equipment. He'd admitted taking only $11,000 worth because he knew he could make good on that much, but not on the larger sum. Acting on advice from Ray and Nard, the store owner refrained from having the clerk arrested but allowed him to make restitution over a period of time.

But the most sensational of all the cases Nard worked on for Ray Schindler was the Sir Harry Oakes murder case in the Bahamas.

It had drama, suspense, and all the ingredients of a prime-time mystery chiller—a colorful setting, a murdered multimillionaire, his pretty daughter, her "fortune-hunting" husband, even a torrential rainstorm the night of the murder. To top it off, the Duke of Windsor (the former Edward VIII of England, who gave up his throne to marry "the woman I love") was then the Royal Governor of the Bahamas.

On the morning of July 8, 1943, in a bedroom of Sir Harry Oakes's luxurious villa outside Nassau, an overnight guest found the knighted multimillionaire's body; the head bludgeoned, the body scorched and singed by fire. It was a gruesome sight.

It was well known that Sir Harry had violently disapproved of the marriage of his eighteen-year-old daughter, Nancy, to twice-married Count Alfred de Marigny, and that he and the Count had been quarreling since. Therefore, the Nassau police arrested de Marigny as their chief suspect and threw him in jail. Many townspeople who had long considered the count a phony and ne'er-do-well were soon convinced of his guilt. They clamored to have him hanged. The investigators for the prosecution, who went about collecting evidence mostly detrimental to the count, also seemed bent on sending de Marigny to the gallows.

At the time of the murder, Lady Oakes and the younger children were vacationing in the United States. Nancy, also in the United States, believed positively that her husband was innocent. Horrified by the growing hostility against him, she called on Ray Schindler for help.

From news accounts, Ray had surmised that de Marigny probably was guilty. To be completely ethical, he told Nancy that if he found any evidence of the count's guilt, he'd have to turn it over to the prosecution. Nancy agreed.

In Nassau, Ray soon learned that Sir Harry, originally an American, had amassed a fortune estimated at $200 million. Later he had become a British citizen and had been knighted by the Crown. In amassing his wealth, he'd made enemies. Ray reasoned there must be many former business associates and acquaintances still around who held grudges. Hoping the police would round up some of these "suspects" to examine on the polygraph, he sent for Nard. But soon after Nard arrived in Nassau with his little black box, he learned that British law banned lie detector tests in court cases. Ray then proposed that

Nard, an all-around criminologist, assist him in investigating de Marigny, hoping that somehow, before the trial ended, Nard would have the chance to run the principals on the lie detector.

Already the case was getting worldwide coverage. De Marigny had been formally indicted, and the trial neared. Detectives, criminologists, reporters, and writers converged on Nassau from all over the United States and Europe. Among them was Erle Stanley Gardner, the mystery writer, who, in the role of Perry Mason, wrote a day-by-day account of the "trial of the century" for a chain of newspapers.

Gathering his news, Gardner soon met up with Ray and Nard. In his first full-page spread, which appeared the day the trial opened, October 18, he wrote: "I have an appointment with the man who has done more, perhaps, than any man living to pry into the guilty secrets of his fellow mortals—Professor Leonarde Keeler, who has pretty much perfected the so-called lie detector. Now Perry Mason knows that Professor Keeler did not come over here for the fishing ... I'm probably not allowed to make a written guess just now as to why he did come, but the intelligent reader can form the same conclusion that Perry Mason is reaching. And so tomorrow I hope to have an article for you on the man who reads minds with a box."

In the next day's article about Nard, Gardner explained that the lie detector did not actually read minds but that "the records prove conclusively that the box plus brains do the trick."

The meeting of Nard, Ray, and Erle Stanley Gardner seemed preordained. Entirely different men, but sharing an intense interest in solving crimes, the three clicked immediately. They talked over the case and the chances of proving de Marigny innocent. Before becoming a writer, Erle had been a lawyer, both for defense and prosecution, and like his new friend, he had a soft spot for the underdog. He offered to help Ray in any way he could. And by his keen deductions and analyses, he did.

Shortly after arriving in Nassau, Ray located documents to prove that Count de Marigny was not a phony but a registered French count; that he had graduated with honors from college and was an athlete; and that, far from being a penniless ne'er-do-well, he owned a prosperous chicken ranch, two homes, and had a substantial bank account.

He learned that on the night of the murder de Marigny had

given a party for about twenty guests in his home, several miles from Sir Harry's villa. When the party broke up, around midnight, he drove two women guests home. On the way he passed near the villa but had not stopped there. About an hour after he returned home, a house guest who had also driven a young lady home returned and parked behind de Marigny's car, blocking it in. The guest went up to his room by an outside stairway.

Using a model of de Marigny's house, the parking area, and the two parked cars, Ray showed the jury that after returning home, de Marigny could not have gone to the villa and murdered his father-in-law without first obtaining his house guest's car keys.

That was only a small portion of Ray's evidence. He also proved that one of de Marigny's two dozen identical shirts had not been bloodstained and disposed of, as the prosecution had contended; that hair on the back of de Marigny's hands had not been burned at the murder scene, but by lighting hurricane lamps.

But the most damaging evidence was a print of de Marigny's little finger that an investigator for the prosecution claimed to have lifted from a scorched screen in the murder room. This fingerprint was the prosecution's most conclusive proof that de Marigny had been in the room at the time of the murder.

Nard's task was to disprove this. He spent hours putting his own fingerprints all over the screen, then sprinkling powder on them and "lifting" them with transparent adhesive tape. By this arduous process, he finally proved (as a fingerprint expert from New Orleans corroborated) that the investigator for the prosecution could not have lifted de Marigny's print from that screen. For on Nard's tapes, showing through all of his prints were little curlicues from the design on the screen. None showed through the de Marigny print.

The murder trial, held in full British pomp, with the judge and barristers wearing robes and white shoulder-length wigs, lasted twenty-two days. During the first two weeks, the prosecution's evidence tightened the noose around de Marigny's neck. But in the final days, Ray Schindler's barrage of facts and exhibits, and particularly Nard's proof that de Marigny's fingerprint could not have been lifted from the screen in the murder room, broke down all the arguments. De Marigny was acquitted.

It was a time of jubilation. But some skeptics still believed de
Marigny guilty and wanted him expelled from the Bahamas. The
night after the trial, the Baron and Baroness Trolle (she had been
a school friend of Nancy's) gave a party for the de Marignys', their
friends, and members of the defense team. Nard was asked to
bring his lie detector. During the festivities he and some of the
guests played card and number games. Guests picked a number
from one to ten, and from their responses on the machine, Nard
told them which number they had chosen.

Intrigued by the never-failing accuracy of the "magic box",
the guests were laughing and chatting when Freddy de Marigny
spoke up: "How about giving me a lie detector test?" A sudden
hush came over the room. Nard looked questioningly at Nancy,
Sir Godfrey Higgs (Freddy's attorney), and Ray Schindler. Their
expressions reassured him. De Marigny continued: "You can ask
me anything you want to know about the murder—just don't ask
me about my past."

Glancing at de Marigny, Nard gestured to the chair by the
polygraph. Tension mounted as the guests gathered around.
Nard started to attach de Marigny to the machine, then paused.
"You wouldn't rather do this quietly, in another room?"

"No, go ahead."

For moments the only sound was the swish of the pens on the
moving graph. In his low, even voice Nard explained the procedures. He knew that even if de Marigny ran a guilty record, he
could not be tried again ... but suspicions would continue. If his
polygram was clear, all doubt should be erased.

As usual, Nard began with nonsensitive questions: "Is your
name Fred?" "Do you live in Nassau?" Then, "When you took
those two ladies home the night of July 7, did you return straight
home?"

"Yes," de Marigny replied.

"Did you enter Westbourne [Sir Harry's villa]?"

"No."

"Have you eaten today?"

"Yes."

"Were you in the room when someone else killed Sir Harry
Oakes?"

"No."

"Did you place your hand on that screen between the time of the murder and the discovery of the body?"

"No."

"Have you been telling the truth?"

"Yes."

Throughout the questioning, the pens traced an even graph, to the relief of all those present, especially Nard and members of the defense team. The next day, news services transmitted the story of de Marigny's "truth test" to papers all over the United States.

Besides the successful outcome of the trial, Nard had made new friends—Erle Stanley Gardner, whom he saw often in the years ahead; the de Marignys; and the Trolles, whom he saw on subsequent occasions. Also, he and Ray Schindler had become much better acquainted.

Ray's only regret was that the Nassau authorities had not permitted him to track down the real murderer. Theories on who had committed the crime ranged from voodoo witch doctors to gangland overlords, but officially the murder of Sir Harry Oakes remains an unsolved mystery to this day.

CHAPTER 24

The Lie Detector In World War II

In April 1944, Uncle Sterling and his wife, Betsy, received a postcard from K. Dussaq. WASP, Headquarters Squadron, Randolph Field, Texas. The picture showed a U. S. Army plane doing a slow roll over Randolph Field. On the back was written:

> Well—it worked. Was on my good behavior 6 weeks and got transferred to the West Point of the Air Corps—Randolph—as a staff pilot. But it may be only temporary. Hope not as I like it a lot. Am getting checked out on twin engine stuff soon.
>
> Regards, Kay

That was the last time any of our family in California heard from Kay. Whether Nard heard from her, I can't say. But surely her exploits in the Air Corps made him more anxious than ever to get in the fray.

By the spring of 1944, he must have about given up. Then a telephone call came from Lt. Col. Ralph Pierce, chief of Scientific Investigations Branch, Fort Sam Houston. Pierce had been authorized by Washington, he explained, to hire Nard to investigate a murder in a large army installation in the Southwest.

"Nard spent about two weeks out there, but came up with the answer," Colonel Pierce wrote me. He continued: "Then we were sent on a very secret case in Tennessee where the atomic bombs were made (in part). We knew, of course, something secret was going on but we didn't know exactly what."

Colonel Pierce beame so interested in the lie detector and Nard's interrogation techniques that he took his course for polygraph examiners and worked with him on numerous army cases, some important to our national security.

In November 1944, Nard visited his good friends in East Lansing, Michigan: Dr. LeMoyne Snyder, his wife, Louise, and their three children.

When Nard and LeMoyne first became acquainted, at the 1933 Chicago World's Fair, LeMoyne was a surgeon who was also studying law. Impressed by the crime lab exhibit, he decided to take the scientific crime detection course at Northwestern. He was in Nard's class. After being admitted to the bar, he combined his interests, eventually becoming the leading medical-legal expert in the U.S. Police officers, coroners, lawyers, and all types of investigators use his book, *Homicide Investigation*. At LeMoyne's recommendation, the Michigan State Police bought one of Nard's polygraphs and hired Harold Mulbar, a friend and trainee of Nard's, to operate it. Nard and LeMoyne worked together on many cases in Michigan and elsewhere.

But one particular Sunday evening during Nard's visit they were just relaxing at home with the family. Nard had been telling about a radio offer he had had, to commute to New York once a week to host a network series based on true stories of his cases.

Then someone turned on the radio. There was a news flash: "Katherine Applegate Dussaq, member of the Woman's Auxiliary Service Pilots—The WASPs—was killed in an airplane crash near Newcastle, Ohio. The army has notified her parents, Mr. and Mrs. A. M. Applegate of Walla Walla, Washington . . . The crash occurred as she was flying blind and attempted a landing after the plane's fuel was exhausted. Mrs. Dussaq, aged thirty-eight, was the former wife of Leonarde Keeler . . .

Nard appeared calm to the Snyders, but when he returned to Chicago and learned more details—how Kay had flown from one airport to another through the dense fog, . . . how she ran out of gas, how ground control told her to bail out, how the bomber crashed and burst into flame—he could no longer control his feelings. In a long-distance call, he poured out his heart to Kay's mother in Walla Walla blaming the tragedy on himself and the divorce.

Unable to console him on the telephone, Mrs. Applegate wrote, urging him to be realistic. Their rivalry had made their divorce inevitable, she insisted, with no real blame on either side.

She reminded him, "Kay loved to live dangerously and, at last, chance caught up with her . . . and perhaps she would not have it otherwise. Remember the lovely things in the relationship. Have no regrets."

But her loving admonition was not easy to follow. Two weeks before Christmas, Nard called me at the radio station where I worked in Sacramento. He was to host a network radio series, he said, and wanted me to write it. He begged me to come to Chicago right away. Then Jane Wilson came on the line, "Please come," she urged.

"Is he terribly upset over Kay?" I asked.

"Yes. He needs you. We all need you. It's terribly important that you come."

So I resigned my job, sold my car, and in a few days was on my way to the Windy City—perhaps, I thought, to fame and fortune as the writer of a network radio series but more likely to comfort a grieving brother.

Charlie and Jane met me at the railroad station and drove

Reunion of Leonarde and Eloise Keeler in 1945 at the Yar Restaurant in Chicago.

me to their apartment. Nard, looking pale and not at all himself, was waiting for us. Jane cooked dinner. Afterward, Nard told me the radio show had been called off. His doctor had convinced him that with his other work, his heart wouldn't take the extra strain. "But don't flip," he cautioned with a trace of his old twinkle. "We'll see that you get a job."

During the war, living space was hard to come by. I stayed with the Wilsons two days, then moved into a small room with bath on the nineteenth floor of the Allerton Hotel, formerly a Y.M.C.A. It was not an auspicious beginning. I didn't know that I could really help Nard. As I gazed around my eight-by-ten-foot quarters, I felt let down, bewildered.

But, as it usually turned out, Nard helped *me*.

Soon I found myself in a whirl of Christmas festivities. His assistants took care of the office while he took time out for the holidays—and to try to forget the shock of Kay's death.

On Christmas morning Nard invited me for breakfast. While he was busy with prepartions, he asked me to answer his telephone. I was impressed; eight women called him before breakfast.

At one of the parties I met an advertising agent who wrote me a letter of recommendation. And after the holidays, I landed a job writing scripts for the *Chicago Tribune's* new FM radio station. Now I was on my own. The FM staff was congenial. I loved my work and soon found my own social group.

Meanwhile, Nard kept working on his cases for the army. Most were secret, at least at that time. But among his papers is a letter to Lt. Col. James Edler that pretty much tells the story:

> We have been exceedingly busy here in the office with our usual routine work on personnel cases, as well as criminal cases, and on top of our regular program we have had considerable army work. Just recently I took eight of our trained operators from various police departments about the country to Fort Getty, Rhode Island, where we screened 270 German war prisoners, who were to be trained as police officers to assist the American Occupational Forces in Germany. It was an extremely interesting project, requiring about three weeks' time. About one third of those chosen for the training group and returned to Germany had to be eliminated after our examination.
>
> I have had other cases in POW camps, all of which were very

interesting. One in particular involved a Nazi, who turned traitor, and gave our armed forces valuable information; was sent to a POW camp where he was promptly strung up by his comrades. Without a clue to work on, within three weeks we had the nine prisoners responsible for the hanging ...

Nard and his colleagues were at Fort Getty when the atomic bombs were dropped on Japan, ending the war in the Pacific. During that time they began to talk about creating a new professional organization. These just stirrings were described later in the inaugural bulletin of the International Society for the Detection of Deception, August 1948:

Several well-known and experienced polygraph operators who had been assembled at Fort Getty for the screening project discussed the desirability of forming an association which could serve as a clearing house for the exchange of experiences and ideas. It was the consensus of all those present that such an organization was highly desirable and that it would promote the efficiency of the detection of deception technique. It was also felt that it would create and maintain a closer working relationship between operators in various parts of the country for the exchange of research data and material. Further, that it would assist in establishing a high standard of ethics and generally increase the prestige of the profession.

The discussion led to action. An organization meeting was held which was attended by W. J. Austin, Leonarde Keeler, Ralph W. Pierce, David Cowles, Charles M. Wilson, Paul Trovillo and Russell Chatham. All of those present, as well as Dr. LeMoyne Snyder and Harold F. Mulbar, became charter members.

At this meeting a committee was appointed to draw up the constitution and bylaws. An election was held at which time the following officers were selected: Colonel Ralph W. Pierce, president David Cowles, vice-president; and W. J. Austin, secretary-treasurer. Leonarde Keeler was elected Chairman of the Board of Directors.

The International Society for the Detection of Deception was formally incorporated at Bismarck, N. D., on December 30, 1947.

The organization's name was later changed to the Academy for Scientific Interrogation. Then John Reid of the Chicago Police

Department started another organization. The two were eventually consolidated into the American Polygraph Association, which today has chapters in every state.

Several months after the mass screening of German war prisoners at Fort Getty, Nard participated in another secret and extremely important project for the U.S. Army. In the *Chicago Tribune* for March 14, 1946, under the headline *LIE DETECTOR USED TO GUARD A-BOMB SECRETS,* it was disclosed that Leonarde Keeler had supervised a staff of lie detector operators testing employees of the atomic bomb plant at Oak Ridge, Tennessee. The Oak Ridge examination took three weeks, and the *Tribune* called it the largest mass operation ever made with a lie detector.

Nard was understandably secretive about the project. But I know that after this mass testing, one member of Nard's special staff, Russell Chatham, was retained on a regular basis at Oak Ridge and continued the examinations over a period of several years.

CHAPTER 25

The Hesse Crown Jewels

One afternoon in May 1946, Nard called me at the FM station. Something would be going on that evening at his apartment, he said. Would I come over? I knew he was pursuing an important case, but I didn't know *how* important. "I'll be there," I told him.

Nard met me at the door of the stately Victorian mansion and ushered me into his living room. Two army officers with pistols in their holsters were milling about, along with some of Nard's business associates and close friends, including LeMoyne and Louise Snyder. As Nard introduced me around, I sensed an air of mystery and excitement. Finally he said, "Come on. I'll show you what's up."

Adjoining his own quarters on the ground floor was a large studio apartment Nard leased for guests. On that memorable evening both apartments were thrown open. He now led me to the front apartment.

Spread out on the large table, desk, divan, and every available surface was an incredible display of jewelry. Most of it was modern—platinum and diamond rings, bracelets, earrings, wrist watches. Some were gold set with rubies, emeralds, and sapphires. There were strings of perfectly matched pearls; a gold table service with handles of jade, lapis lazuli, carnelian, and other semiprecious stones; a large Bible with embossed covers of solid gold. The Bible had belonged to Queen Victoria and it recorded the births of her children. And there were many other priceless heirlooms, each bearing an identification tag.

Nard explained that the treasures had just been brought

from Wisconsin, of all unlikely places, where they'd been hidden in the attic of a farmhouse. Colonel Ralph Pierce and Major John D. Salb, the two army officers, were taking inventory as we gazed on. It was one of the largest jewel heists in the history of crime— the work of American Military personnel tempted to become looters, or "souvenir collectors," in enemy territory at the end of World War II. In this case, the souvenirs collected were treasures of most of the royal families of Europe.

Briefly, here is the story of these jewels:

Friedrichshof, an eighty-room, turreted castle near Kronberg, Germany, had been captured by the U.S. Army, which used it as a recreation center for officers on leave. In charge was a forty-three-year-old captain in the Women's Army Corps (WAC). One day, bored and hearing that bottles of rare old wine were stashed away in the castle, some of the officers started to search for them. Eventually, in a subcellar, they came upon a row of bottles. While the men drank and made merry in the halls above, one corporal who remained in the subcellar noticed a hole in the floor where the bottles had been. In that hole he discovered a lead-lined box containing the royal treasure.

Immediately he informed the WAC captain. After swearing the corporal to secrecy, the WAC said she would take care of it.

By this time the war was over. Troops were being sent home. Most of the officers at the castle were on terminal leave—they could go home, but could still be recalled to active duty within a specified period. Soon after the discovery of the jewels, the WAC captain took off for the United States with a close friend, Colonel D., who had been stationed in nearby Frankfurt and had often visited the castle.

The owner of Friedrichshof, or Kronberg Castle, as it was more generally called, resumed residence. She was the seventy-four-year-old Princess Margareta of the German House of Hesse, the sister of Kaiser Wilhelm II. While her castle had been used as what she termed a *Bierhalle,* she had "existed" in a nearby eight-room cottage.

Now it happened that Princess Margareta's widowed daughter-in-law, Princess Sophie von Hesse, was about to remarry. She asked her mother-in-law to return her jewels to wear at the wedding. But the jewels were nowhere to be found.

When Princess Margareta inquired at the castle for the WAC

captain in charge, she was informed she had left. The captain who had replaced her, and the officers still at the castle, knew nothing about the jewels. All they found in the subcellar were a litter of empty wine bottles and an empty hole in the floor.

Since the jewels were valued at around $3 million, and relatives had sent many of them to Princess Margareta for safekeeping during the war, she complained to the U.S. Army and demanded their recovery.

The Army's Criminal Investigation Division, with Colonel Pierce as chief, set to work immediately; the case involved not only the royal families of our former enemies, but also those of our allies. Prime suspects were the WAC captain and Colonel D. Shortly after their arrival in the United States, they had been married—presumably so they couldn't testify against each other.

The WAC captain had left several forwarding addresses, and she was soon traced to her sister's home, on a Wisconsin farm. But as MPs arrived at the house, she escaped by the back door.

Informed that Colonel D. was in Chicago and expecting his bride to join him there, the investigators called the leading hotels. The WAC's terminal leave had already expired. (Except for fraud against the government, military personnel at that time could not be charged after their discharge with crimes they had committed while in service.) But as letters ordering her back to active duty had been sent to all her forwarding addresses, she could be apprehended for being AWOL.

Through the phone calls, the investigators found the fugitives had registered as Colonel and Mrs. D. at the LaSalle Hotel in Chicago. At 2 a.m. the next morning, bride and groom were awakened by MPs who took them to nearby Fort Sheridan. The colonel's leave had not yet expired. They were both under arrest.

The following day, the WAC was brought to Nard's office, which had become headquarters for the investigation. (Luckily for her, for a day or two later, fire ravaged the floor in the hotel where she and her husband had stayed, killing most of the occupants.) After being introduced to the WAC, Nard talked to her for a while. They became friendly. Then, with her consent, he attached her to the polygraph. With Colonel Pierce and Major Salb looking on, he started his test. After the usual preliminaries, he asked: "Do you know who stole the jewels from Kronberg Castle? Do you know where the jewels are now? Did you participate in the theft?" And so on down a list of prepared questions. To each one the WAC answered no. But on the graph her responses became increasingly marked, indicating she was not telling the truth.

After repeating the tests with the same results, Nard asked another set of questions that included: "Did you hide some of the jewels at your sister's home in Wisconsin?" Although the WAC replied in the negative, her emotional response gave her away, and she knew it.

In further questioning off the detector, she confessed to the entire caper. Her accomplices, she said, had been Colonel D., another major who was still in Germany, and a sergeant who had already returned to civilian life. She had some of the jewels, her husband had others, but she didn't know where the rest were. She gave Colonel Pierce a letter to her sister in Wisconsin that contained a code word they'd agreed on, "commanding" her to turn the jewels over to the agents who called for them.

Those jewels and heirlooms, valued at close to a million dollars, were the ones in Nard's front apartment. To our astonishment, he told those gathered that the sister had worn some of the jewels to a country dance and had used the gold table service at meals in the farmhouse kitchen. He also told us that the sergeant involved had sent $50,000 worth of the jewels to a girl friend in Ireland.

Within the next few days, Colonel D. was brought in and asked to take a lie detector test. He cheerfully agreed, claiming he knew nothing about the theft and had nothing to hide. But his polygram indicated deception and that he probably knew where the remaining jewels were hidden. Still, hours of interrogation off the detector by Colonel Pierce and Major Salb—and later LeMoyne Snyder—failed to elicit a confession.

Days later, while Colonel Pierce was wearily repeating the questions off the polygraph, Colonel D. finally heaved a deep sigh. The strain had become too great. He was ready to talk. But first he asked to make a phone call—privately. Afterward he explained that he'd be called back at a pay telephone in a certain restaurant. Accompanied by the investigators, he received the call on schedule, then proceeded to a locker at a railway station. Unlocking it, he drew out a cardboard box. It was stuffed with gems.

The suspects had been working with a dealer in stolen goods.

The gems had been knocked out of crowns worn by European monarchs, and the crowns, some of great historic value, had been melted down for their gold.

Although he refused to name his fence, Colonel D. claimed he'd been double-crossed, for some of the largest stones were missing.

Several months later, Nard traveled to Washington, D.C., and then to Germany to testify at the trials. Three of the culprits—the WAC captain, Colonel D., and the major—were dishonorably discharged, sent to prison, and paroled after relatively short terms. The sergeant had already returned to civilian life and so could not be prosecuted.

Princess Sophie did not get back her jewels in time for her wedding, but the remaining jewels and heirlooms were eventually returned to her mother-in-law, Princess Margareta, proud owner of Kronberg Castle.

CHAPTER 26

The Last Years

By the end of World War II, Nard was at the peak of his career — handsome, famous, sought-after, prospering, with an unlimited future. But his high blood pressure (for which in those days there was no medication) was an ever-present danger, and underneath his genial self, he sometimes seemed deeply depressed. Kay's death haunted him, and he still received vengeful threats from the sister of the Illinois man who'd been executed in 1937 after a lie test. And the daily strain of running cases on the polygraph did not let up. Most people, I'm sure, were unaware of his condition. And despite his health problems, his last three years continued to be productive and adventurous.

While the crown jewel case was going on, Louise Snyder, who thought she had accompanied her husband to Chicago for a vacation, was so fascinated by the splendor of it all that she stayed around for a few days to help in the investigation. But after the loose gems were found in the railway locker, Louise returned to East Lansing, and LeMoyne and Nard took off on a delayed vacation to Southern California.

On the way they stopped over in Santa Fe to see two of Nard's artist friends — he'd become quite a connoisseur of art — then continued on to Los Angeles to attend a cocktail party for top movie stars given by Ray Schindler, who was planning to open a branch office in Beverly Hills.

Nard, LeMoyne, and Ray all stayed at the Jonathon Club, a big men's club resembling a hotel. Erle Stanley Gardner had invited them to his ranch in Temecula, across a mountain range

Nard with friends and associates at Yar Restaurant.

from Palm Springs, but first Nard wanted to look up some friends
at the L.A. Police Department.

When the director of the L.A. crime lab and the chief of
homicide heard the three famous criminologists were in town,
they invited them and several fellow police officers to lunch — but
not just for a social get-together. They'd been working on a
baffling case — a murder, they thought — and they had a possible
suspect. They wanted Nard, LeMoyne, and Ray to help.

The wife of a nurseryman who lived out in the valley some
twenty miles from downtown Los Angeles had mysteriously
disappeared. But rather than paraphrase it, I'll let LeMoyne
Snyder tell the story himself, as he recorded it on tape some years
later:

Well, this nurseryman fellow reported to the police that his wife
was gone. He didn't know where, but had all sorts of ideas. The
police made an investigation, sent out bulletins, but they didn't
find anything.

It seems the couple had a grown daughter who had left home, but
with her father there alone she'd come back to stay with him, at

least for a few days. She'd started tidying up the house, dusting, sweeping, and so on, when under the bed her parents had slept in she found her mother's partial denture containing her front teeth. As the daughter knew her mother wouldn't even answer the front door without her denture, she reported her find to the police.

The police admitted this looked suspicious. But after further investigations they still hadn't been able to get anyplace and the case had dragged on for several months.

Well, at that luncheon Nard, Ray, and I had quite a talk with the police officials and finally suggested the way to handle this nurseryman fellow was to get a little rough — go out to his place in the middle of the night, pick him up, bring him downtown, and throw him in jail. And we'd talk to him the next day.

So they did that. And the following morning the three of us went over to the police department to try to get this fellow on the polygraph. But he'd have no part of it — said he had a bad heart and "this thing" wouldn't work on anybody with a bad heart. I examined his heart and it was all right. But although we fooled around there all day, we couldn't get him within two rods of the polygraph.

Around five o'clock Nard, Ray, and I decided to go back to the Jonathon Club. The detectives we'd been working with said, "We'll call you. Don't worry! He'll go on the polygraph."

Well, we hadn't been back at the club half an hour when we got a call: "He'll take the test!" They'd somehow talked him into it.

So after dinner the three of us went back to the police department. Nard gave the fellow several tests on the polygraph, and inside of twenty minutes he had the whole story — that he'd strangled his wife and buried her out by the greenhouse. When he'd finished the test, Nard said something like, "Now don't you think we should go out there and dig her up — give her a decent funeral?"

The fellow's eyes sort of filled up. "Let's go!" he said.

So we started out. Had quite a caravan — three or four cars — policemen, reporters, photographers. It was pitch dark. Along the way we stopped at a fire station to pick up electric torches and shovels, and finally we drove into the fellow's place — walked with him into his greenhouse, where he turned on the lights, then out a side door to some sort of vegetable plot — a squash patch, I think — and it was covered with about an inch of flowing water. He pointed to a spot in the middle of the water and said, "Here's the place." Thinking he was just giving us a bad time, I told him, "Now look, we're not out here to play games. If you say that's where the body is, it had better be there or there's going to be trouble." "It's there," he said.

So several of the L.A. policemen took off their shoes and socks, rolled up their trousers, and, after using shovels to divert the stream of water, began to dig. It was a muddy hog wallow. The rest of us held flashlights so they could see. And by golly, they kept on digging and finally came upon her fur coat. Underneath it was the body.

The fellow was convicted and sentenced to be executed in the gas chamber at San Quentin. But later that was canceled. As he was a skilled nurseryman, they put him in charge of the prison grounds — flower beds, that sort of thing. And after not too long a time — six or seven years, I think — they finally let him go.

It turned out he'd been a pretty nice guy but had been nagged by his wife until he could no longer endure it. He'd buried her fur coat with her so people would think she'd gone away.

Nard, LeMoyne, and Ray finally reached Erle's ranch, hours late. Their host was irked, until they told him of the macabre adventure that had held them up.

Nard visited Erle several times in Temecula. In the course of their meetings there and in Chicago, he often discussed his work. Erle was particularly interested in cases in which Nard had helped free wrongfully committed prisoners. I've already described some such cases, such as the prisoner who raised canaries, but the most famous concerned a man named Joe Majczek (pronounced May-check), convicted of slaying a police officer.

For eleven years Majczek's mother scrubbed floors in a Chicago skyscraper to earn the money for a reward she believed would free her son from prison. Through a newspaper ad, she offered $5,000 for the names of the real killer or killers. The story appeared in various publications, including the *Reader's Digest*. In 1948 it was made into a movie, *Call Northside 777,* starring Jimmy Stewart as the newspaper reporter who investigates the case. Nard was also in the film, playing himself. Besides its entertainment value, the film neatly illustrates the workings of the polygraph. For example, following one of Majczek's polygraph tests, Nard and Jimmy Stewart are looking over Majczek's polygram. Jimmy asks: "What's that jump there?"

Nard. He lied to that question.

Jimmy. Is that where you asked if he killed someone?

Nard. No. I asked, "Are you married?"

Jimmy. But he didn't lie. He isn't married — he's divorced.

Nard. Yes, but he's a Catholic. He still thinks he's married, and in his mind he feels himself married, so he reacted.

Around the time this picture came out, Erle Stanley Gardner started a project called the Court of Last Resort, to reinvestigate cases of wrongfully condemned prisoners. Among the experts he asked to participate were LeMoyne Snyder, Ray Schindler, and Nard. Nard assisted in the planning, but his illness kept him from participating in the actual cases. One of his skilled and competent assistants served in his place. Through the years, the Court has saved many lives of innocent men and brought freedom to unjustly convicted prisoners.

Meantime, Nard had traveled to Germany for the Hesse Crown Jewels trials and then to the Dominican Republic. There he was in an automobile accident. The chauffeur-driven car he was riding in went over an embankment. In addition to cuts and bruises, Nard sustained several broken ribs and a dislocated wrist. I clearly remember, when he was finally back at his apartment, how solicitously his lady friends cared for him.

Nard often thought about remarrying, but claimed he hadn't met the right person. From what I saw, he seldom took out women alone; usually a crowd went along. I can still see him one night when a young mother arrived at his apartment with her two grown daughters. After embracing each, he stood back in admiration, exclaiming, "You're all three so beautiful. I don't know which one I'm in love with!" Another time, there was a bright, attractive nineteen-year-old who told him right out she wanted to marry him. When, with characteristic bluntness, he replied, "Sorry, I can't marry you. I have only a year to live;" she parried with, "I'd rather be married to you for a year than to any other man for a lifetime." In fact, the two women he cared for most were the two he needed most — Olie Stevens, who took care of his office and business appointments, and Jane Wilson, who ran polygraph tests. Both also served as social secretaries.

By the summer of 1947, the Cold War had started, with its

subversive activities and spy scares. More and more government agencies and branches of the armed forces bought Keeler Polygraphs and sent future operators to Nard to be trained. More than ever, he needed bigger quarters, more assistants, and a longer, more comprehensive training course. His friend Walter Podbielniak, the chemist, who had recently bought a four-story building on Ohio Street, offered to lease him an entire floor. Because of his precarious health, I thought the move would be too great a strain and I urged Nard not to take it.

He was still trying to make up his mind when Charlie Wilson accepted a new job — setting up and directing a crime lab in Madison for the state of Wisconsin. Charlie, Jane, and their son, Mike, were still Nard's closest friends. Their leaving Chicago was a blow. Fortunately, there would be a lot of traveling back and forth between Chicago and Madison.

On one of Nard's visits to the Wilsons, they were all sitting around when the front door opened and a beautiful young woman walked in. Nard gasped. It was Kay! He went white, until Jane spoke up: "You know who this is, Nard — Clemmy, Kay's younger sister. I should have told you she was coming." Clemmy was the image of Kay, except younger and more beautiful.

Nard got along famously with Mike, then around ten. He enjoyed children greatly. An amateur magician, he'd amuse them by making objects vanish and taking coins out of their ears. And he'd delight them with tales of mountain-climbing expeditions and strange "pets."

Fascinated by one of Nard's animal stories, Pixie, six years old and the Snyders' youngest child, begged him to bring her a "reptile." So on his next visit, he brought several fanciful rubber lizards and snakes — which Pixie scorned. They weren't real! "Pixie, I'll tell you what," Nard said. "I'll send you a couple of bull snakes. They're gentle, clean, you can let them loose in the house, and they'll take care of all your rats and mice."

Overhearing this conversation, Louise thought it just talk — until a week or two later, Nard telephoned from Chicago to say he'd found a couple of bull snakes at a pet store. They were being shipped.

With sudden visions of snakes slithering along her mantel, Louise gulped. "Nard, we don't have any rats or mice. The snakes, I'm afraid, wouldn't be happy here. They're not exactly suitable.

Nard, you'll have to cancel the shipment" — for which Pixie, now a beautiful woman in her thirties, has never forgiven her mother.

By the summer of 1947, I decided to leave Chicago. I'd already given notice at the radio station when word came from California that our stepmother had died of a heart attack. Nard left immediately to help Merodine, and a few days later I followed. As Merodine and I sorted our family possessions in the ensuing weeks, I decided this was the time to buy a home of my own. Before long I found a cottage on a wooded hillside overlooking San Francisco.

Concurrently, Nard wrote that he was moving his business to the Ohio Street address. His expanded, six-week course was an immediate success. His regular business of screening employees and job applicants was thriving. He and his assistants still worked on criminal cases.

But the big demand in this period was for loyalty tests, controversial then and now. Despite a barrage of criticism, particularly from liberal groups and labor unions, Nard and his assistants helped to preserve our national security at a crucial period in our history through these tests.

During the next year and a half, Nard and I were in close contact. He often telephoned; we had recording machines and sent records back and forth; twice he came out to visit. He seemed to need his relatives.

In December 1947, he was coming west on a crack train, the City of San Francisco, and was recording a long newsy letter about his trip to the gang at his office. But Nard didn't get to San Francisco on time. That night, according to the UP press release, "Five miles west of Great Salt Lake the streamliner City of San Francisco jumped the tracks and rolled across the flat desert terrain. All 15 cars of the train remained upright. All of the passengers escaped serious injury . . .

Nard was unhurt, but was badly shaken up when he called to tell us what had happened. When finally Merodine, her teenage daughters, an aunt, uncle, and I met him at the station, he was still keyed up. Twice within a year he'd narrowly escaped disaster.

As usual on his trips west, he called on August Vollmer, now retired. The chief was living in North Berkeley, cared for by a housekeeper. His wife had died and his health had failed, but his

Reunion of "The Three Musketeers" — from L., Elwood Woolsey,
Leonarde Keeler, Ralph Brandt.

mind remained keen and alert. He was writing a book and
conferring with criminologists from all over the country. As
always, he was delighted to see Nard and to hear about his work.
If Vollmer noticed any change in his disciple, he never mentioned
it. But he did urge Nard to be sure to see O. W. Wilson.

After a tour of duty in the European theater, O. W., the
former Wichita police chief, was back in Berkeley. Assisted by
Chief Vollmer, he had organized and was directing the first
School of Criminology at the University of California. (Later O.
W. became the commissioner of police in Chicago.)

The day I drove Nard to his home, O. W. offered him a job
teaching at the new school. Nard wanted to accept. He admitted
to me later that it might have saved his life. He liked my cottage,
he wanted a house of his own, to be with friends he'd grown up
with, hills, trees, the bay. But there were too many strings, too

many demands, people depending on him in Chicago. Besides, there was his health. Regretfully, he declined O. W.'s offer.

We had a family Christmas. Then Nard returned to the big, bustling metropolis on the shores of Lake Michigan.

The following year he came out again, but on this trip he spent most of his time in a hospital. The doctor who attended him recommended an operation called a sympathectomy of the spine, "to interrupt part of the nerve pathway of the sympathetic or involuntary nervous system." The operation had helped others, but there were risks. Uncle Sterling, who by then specialized almost exclusively in surgery of the hand, was not overly enthusiastic. Nard put off the operation.

Leaving the hospital, he spent several days in San Francisco with Uncle Sterling, his wife, Betsy, and his youngest relative, Sterling Bunnell, Jr., then about thirteen. Nard and Sterling, Jr., had much in common — love for the wilderness and fascination with strange creatures. Young Sterling's favorite pet was a fairly large South American iguana.

While in California, Nard had his Chicago apartment refurbished, and after visiting the Bunnells, he returned to newly decorated quarters where his party-going friends soon congregated, and to a business more hectic than ever — with hordes of policemen, army officers, and government officials enrolled in his course, tramping in and out. During 1948, Col. Ralph Pierce resigned from the army and joined the staff of Leonarde Keeler, Inc. This was a great break. During the last months of Nard's life, Colonel Pierce, assisted by Olie, took virtual charge of the office.

In the spring of 1949, I was sent to Paris with another woman to gather information for American radio shows on food, fashions, entertainment, protest rallies, poodles. I'd been over there only a short time when Nard wrote that he, LeMoyne, and Erle Stanley Gardner would see me that summer. They were planning a fabulous European tour.

Near the end of May, one of Nard's courses had just ended. He'd put on a big banquet for the students and guest instructors. He was tired. He needed a rest. LeMoyne, who taught the class in homicide investigation, invited him to East Lansing over Memorial Day weekend. He'd been there a day or two, visiting with the family and lazing about, when he complained of seeing double. He hurried back to Chicago, where his friend, Dr. Jack, immediately put him in the hospital. He'd had a slight stroke. After two weeks he was sufficiently recovered to go to the Mayo Clinic, where he remained for a month. Doctors there told him he'd have to cancel his trip.

Adrift, troubled, he again stayed with Louise Snyder and the children, and from there went to visit the Wilsons at their summer cottage near Sturgeon Bay, Wisconsin.

That's where it happened.

Olie wrote the distressing news. Nard had had a massive stroke and had been taken by ambulance to a hospital in Sturgeon Bay. Olie had gone up to be with him. At forty-five years of age, he was paralyzed; couldn't move, couldn't speak; just as the sister of the condemned prisoner had prophesied twelve years earlier.

Two weeks later Olie telephoned. "He's gone."

Many of the get-well cards Nard received and the letters of condolence that came after his death, were from prisoners and guards at Joliet Penitentiary.

Merodine and I stayed on at Nard's apartment to settle his affairs. Later I moved into the front apartment, where the crown jewels had been displayed.

Gradually I became acquainted with Jack La Frandre, the writer-producer of a weekly operetta series, "The Chicago Theatre of the Air." Jack suggested doing a weekly radio series about Nard and his cases. The series, "The Hidden Truth," was broadcast by WGN, the *Chicago Tribune* radio station, over some five hundred stations of the Mutual Network. I prepared the material for each broadcast from Nard's files. Olie and Colonel Pierce helped pick out the most dramatic cases, and Jack La Frandre wrote the dramatizations. Jack adhered to the truth about Nard and his polygraph techniques, but as for the stories, many were more fiction than fact. Perhaps it was just as well: the series ran successfully for two years.

Meanwhile, Nard's business was sold. And though they have changed hands since, Leonarde Keeler, Inc. and the Keeler Polygraph Institute remain in continuous operation. Today they are directed by Leonard Harrelson, at 5906 Milwaukee Avenue, Chicago, Illinois 60646.

The patents on the Keeler Polygraph had run out shortly
before Nard died, and since then, many different instruments
have been manufactured. While his model is no longer produced,
many specimens of it are still in use.

The urn containing Nard's ashes is at the Chapel of the
Chimes in Oakland, California, bearing the simple inscription:

YE SHALL KNOW THE TRUTH